Praise for _Navigating the Minefield_:

"Having worked with Paul both in person and at workshops across the globe, I've found him to be an incredibly insightful individual. Paul has the rare ability to bridge varying points of view within a room, find the commonality, and carry the debate forward through insight and ingenuity. Patricia's experience working through the U.S. Nuclear Regulatory Commission is a fascinating read, and draws the depth of both knowledge management and an engineering background to the fore. This combination is felt throughout the read, and the incredible experience and expertise both Patricia and Paul bring is felt throughout the pages. The breadth of scope covered is truly compelling, illustrating not just innovative approaches towards cost savings and efficiencies from an organizational knowledge sharing sense, but also quality of life, quality of culture, and in a very literal sense, saving lives as illustrated through narrative regarding the U.S. Army. _Navigating the Minefield_ is a fascinating read, and a must for the global knowledge professional."

Eric Hunter
Director of Knowledge, Technology & Innovation Strategies,
Bradford & Barthel, LLP
and Executive Director, Spherical Models, LLC

"Whether you are starting out in KM or have more KM experience, there is something for you in this KM companion. Some of the ideas were new to me and I found much to inspire my own KM efforts. It's good to learn lessons from other KMers, learning from both good and bad KM experiences.

What I like about this companion is that it has a range of realistic up-to-date examples both on how to start KM in an organisation and also how to sustain KM. The examples are drawn from 19 KM programmes from diverse organisations, from government and industry sectors from across the world, and provide great stories to encourage KM in organisations. There are useful anecdotes that you can reuse to sell KM in your organisation."

Karen McFarlane
CILIP Trustee, CILIP Board Chair
Former UK Government Head of Profession for
Knowledge and Information Management

"Books purporting to educate on the multi-dimensional subject of knowledge management often tend to polarise, over-emphasising the near-religious philosophical aspects of the discipline or over-engineering the technology driven tools and techniques.

Eng and Corney have approached the subject from a practical perspective, looking through a selection of concise case studies for what works and what does not across an array of organisations worldwide. That their subject matter comes from multiple sectors across an international pool of organisations with clear multicultural challenges makes the stories documented that much more interesting and useful. As someone who set up the first massively successful knowledge management functions at one of the world's most prominent but risk-averse global financial institutions in its 150-year history, the challenges documented by Eng and Corney and their resolution recommendations resonate. As someone who now has to craft global business strategies by relying on the mature KM solutions of one of the world's most successful consulting firms, the pain points and road blocks highlighted make perfect sense.

A quick and easy read, *Navigating the Minefield* is not a tome meant to outdo War and Peace, but rather is an easy read and a handy reference guide to everyday KM practitioner problems and practical, implementable solutions. A copy of it will sit within easy reach on my desk."

Larry Campbell
Head of Financial Services Strategy, KPMG
Former Group Chief Knowledge Officer, HSBC

"I first met Patricia Eng when she was describing her KM program at the NRC at KM World in 2009 and was blown away by her candor, her common sense, and her ferocious determination to deliver value. I have worked with Paul Corney on numerous occasions and have always been impressed by his ability to take a strategic, balanced view, followed by an unerring ability to get to the heart of the matter. KM practitioners go deep, KM consultants go broad. When you get an alliance between the two, and then add their formidable personal networks, you get something quite extraordinary. This is an unparalleled distillation of learning and wisdom from multiple continents and organisation types, on how to go about implementing KM. It should be required reading for KM practitioners (and consultants), those who are new and those who want to reflect on their practice."

Patrick Lambe
Partner, Straits Knowledge

"Whether you are new to knowledge management or a seasoned KMer, *Navigating the Minefield* is an absolute must-read. Chockablock with time-tested techniques and sage advice, this book simplifies the rather complex domain of managing organizational knowledge. Unlike many books in the field, *Navigating the Minefield* offer solutions that will work in practice, and not just in theory!"

John P. Girard, Ph.D.
Peyton Anderson Endowed Chair
Middle Georgia State University

Navigating
the Minefield

Also available from ASQ Quality Press:

Making Change in Complex Organizations
George K. Strodtbeck III

We Move Our Own Cheese!: A Business Fable About Championing Change
Victor E. Sower And Frank K. Fair

*The Joy of Lean: Transforming, Leading, and Sustaining a
Culture of Engaged Team Performance*
Dodd Starbird

The Certified Six Sigma Green Belt Handbook, Second Edition
Roderick A. Munro, Govindarajan Ramu, and Daniel J. Zrymiak

The Quality Toolbox, Second Edition
Nancy R. Tague

Root Cause Analysis: Simplified Tools and Techniques, Second Edition
Bjørn Andersen and Tom Fagerhaug

*The Certified Manager of Quality/Organizational Excellence Handbook,
Fourth Edition*
Russell T. Westcott, editor

The Certified Six Sigma Black Belt Handbook, Second Edition
T.M. Kubiak and Donald W. Benbow

The ASQ Auditing Handbook, Fourth Edition
J.P. Russell, editor

*The ASQ Quality Improvement Pocket Guide: Basic History, Concepts, Tools,
and Relationships*
Grace L. Duffy, editor

To request a complimentary catalog of ASQ Quality Press
publications, call 800-248-1946, or visit our Web site at
http://www.asq.org/quality-press.

Navigating the Minefield

A Practical KM Companion

Patricia Lee Eng and Paul J. Corney

ASQ Quality Press
Milwaukee, Wisconsin

American Society for Quality, Quality Press, Milwaukee, WI 53203
© 2017 by ASQ.
All rights reserved. Published 2017.
Printed in the United States of America.

22 21 20 19 18 17   5 4 3 2 1

Library of Congress Cataloging-in-Publication Data
Names: Eng, Patricia Lee, author. | Corney, Paul J., author.
Title: Navigating the minefield: a practical KM companion / by Patricia Lee Eng and Paul J. Corney.
Description: Milwaukee, WI: ASQ Quality Press, [2017] | Includes bibliographical references and index.
Identifiers: LCCN 2017005316 | ISBN 9780873899543 (hardcover: alk. paper)
Subjects: LCSH: Knowledge management.
Classification: LCC HD30.2 .E539 2017 | DDC 658.4/038—dc23
LC record available at https://lccn.loc.gov/2017005316

Director, Quality Press and Programs: Ray Zielke
Managing Editor: Paul Daniel O'Mara
Sr. Creative Services Specialist: Randy L. Benson

ASQ Mission: The American Society for Quality advances individual, organizational, and community excellence worldwide through learning, quality improvement, and knowledge exchange.

Attention Bookstores, Wholesalers, Schools, and Corporations: ASQ Quality Press books, video, audio, and software are available at quantity discounts with bulk purchases for business, educational, or instructional use. For information, please contact ASQ Quality Press at 800-248-1946, or write to ASQ Quality Press, P.O. Box 3005, Milwaukee, WI 53201-3005.

To place orders or to request ASQ membership information, call 800-248-1946. Visit our Web site at www.asq.org/quality-press.

♾ Printed on acid-free paper

Quality Press
600 N. Plankinton Ave.
Milwaukee, WI 53203-2914
E-mail: authors@asq.org

The Global Voice of Quality®

Dedication

Researching and creating this book has taken a significant effort over a couple of years. If we have any regrets, it is that our fathers will not be around to see it published. John and Harry passed within six months of each other in August 2015 and February 2016, respectively. Both were great supporters of our careers and it felt appropriate, while recognising the help and support we've had from those close to us, to dedicate this book to our fathers who taught us to work hard, be honest, try to make things better, and always question why things are the way they are.

– Patricia and Paul

Contents

List of Figures

Acknowledgements

We would like to thank our interviewees, all of whom gave selflessly of their time and expertise to enable us to write this book. All of them were open and forthcoming about their successes, challenges, and roadblocks. Without their honesty and candor, we could not have gleaned the insights into the intricacies of "doing" KM that we did. Nor would we have been able to examine and break down the KM program progression and understand the various steps and stages one must go through to build a successful KM program. Frankly, we couldn't have done this without them. Our interviewees are listed below in alphabetical order by last name. Our heartfelt thanks.

– Paul and Patricia

Dominique Poole Avery
Filip Callewaert
Jill Garcia
Stan Garfield
Louise Lai Pei Hsien
Aain Ismail
Sofia Layton
Nick Milton
Ngawai Moss
Helen Mullinder
Rafi Oghoubian
Mike Prevou
Murni Shariff
Arthur Shelley
Simone Staiger Rivas
Gordon Vala Webb

1

About This Book

"I want to write a book to provide the resources that I wish I had had when I started in KM — to help others in their KM efforts wherever they are."

P. ENG

"If even one KM program is saved by a decision maker reading this book and realizing the value of KM, our efforts will have been worthwhile."

P. CORNEY

This book, *Navigating the Minefield: A Practical KM Companion,* was written for anyone who is interested in making more efficient and effective use of knowledge. This knowledge can be their own, that of the teams in which they work, or the knowledge of the wider communities and teams in which they participate.

Whether you are a recently appointed knowledge management (KM) staffer, an experienced 'KMer' who feels stagnant and stuck, or a senior manager with KM oversight responsibility who is looking for ways to improve the use of knowledge in your organization, this book was written for you.

It is always a good idea to seek advice from people who have gone before you. That is why there are so many cookbooks and "how to" videos on the Internet. In most professions, "newbies" are encouraged to learn from journeyman practitioners; later, when they are ready to understand the nuances of performing or creating something, from master craftsmen. It is the same with KM.

The book is based on interviews with individuals from around the world who have created and managed successful KM programs for the companies in which they work. We have examined their KM programs and compiled quotes, insights, and anecdotes from these interviews to show why these programs are successful and how they work to improve both knowledge capture and knowledge flow.

KM PROGRAMS WE LOOKED AT

We examined KM programs at the following organizations (in alphabetical order):

- Airbus
- ARUP
- British Petroleum (BP)
- Cadbury Schweppes
- Defense Acquisition University
- Digital Equipment
- Hewlett Packard
- Intellectual Property Office of Singapore (IPOS)
- International Center for Tropical Agriculture (CIAT)
- Lloyds Register Marine
- Malaysia Petroleum Management (PETRONAS)
- NASA
- Ontario Workplace Safety and Insurance Board (WSIB)
- Port of Antwerp
- Sellafield Ltd.
- Shell Oil
- U.K. National Health Service Digital (NHS Digital), formerly the Health and Social Care Information Centre (HSCIC)
- U.S. Army
- U.S. Nuclear Regulatory Commission (USNRC)

Our interviewees came from five continents and included government and non-government organizations. In the interviews we asked each of them:

- how they built their programs,
- what made their programs work,
- what were their biggest challenges,
- what they would tell a newbie,

- what they would have done differently, and
- what advice and/or reading recommendations they would give to KM newbies.

The book is structured to mimic the "life cycle" of a KM program as follows...

Chapter 2 discusses the various drivers for creating a KM program (the reasons why the organization is pursuing KM) and discusses the factors and considerations one should think about when designing a KM program. As many KM professionals have discovered, if one doesn't examine the initial state of the organization, understand its mission and its knowledge challenges, even the best KM tactics and program intentions are more likely to fail.

Chapter 3 begins with an example that illustrates the cost of not managing organizational knowledge wisely, followed by case studies of KM tactics that our interviewees used to successfully address specific knowledge needs. Examples from government, non-governmental organizations (NGOs), an educational institution, and private industry are used to demonstrate how simple KM tactics can improve employee morale and improve organizational effectiveness in a variety of situations.

Chapter 4 examines how KM changes the way an organization functions. As a company continues to actively support KM and promote KM tactics throughout its organization, the impact of KM broadens from improving specific processes to influencing business operations. What started as a small localized initiative subsequently changed how these companies manage their knowledge assets, resulting in a competitive edge in the marketplace

Chapter 5 speaks to KM programs that have faltered. Unfortunately, not all KM programs enjoy sustained success. All our interviewees noted that it is a constant challenge to keep KM vibrant and alive. Several of our interviewees watched their initially successful KM programs wither and die or go onto life support, surviving only in small pockets within the organization. While sad, the circumstances surrounding the decline of these KM programs can provide insight on ways to keep a KM program going.

In Chapter 6 we discuss the programs we admire. These programs show a strong management commitment to KM and an in-depth understanding of KM's effectiveness as a valuable business tool that is vital to the health of the company.

In Chapter 7 we discuss the things that surprised us as we digested the information gathered from the interviews. We learned some things that we didn't expect and present ten observations we made as we analyzed the interviews in detail. Some of these observations might be helpful to other KMers as they continue to advance their KM programs.

In Chapter 8 we introduce and define the term "knowledgeur" and provide Paul's eight "ates" for your consideration. The "ates" are skills we believe a KMer should have or develop during their KM journey. Note that these are learned skills and that there are many resources out there to help you familiarize yourself with these skills and how to use them.

There are two appendices. The first discusses considerations when hiring a consultant from two different points of view. The second documents the method we used to write this book. We also include a glossary that we hope is helpful to the reader.

All in all, we hope this is a book you are able to refer to when you are trying to find a new perspective or initiative to start or rejuvenate your KM program; a book that prompts you to experiment, and a book that becomes a reliable companion throughout your KM journey.

If even one KM program is saved by a decision maker reading this book and realizing the value of KM, our efforts will have been worthwhile.

2

Surveying the Minefield

Most companies worry about losing people but they rarely worry about losing knowledge. Despite increased global communications capabilities, experts remain in their organizational silos and often take their in-depth expertise with them when they leave—sometimes going to their company's competitors. When critical knowledge walks out the door, organizations can lose their competitive edge and wind up reinventing wheels that had been rolling smoothly for years.

Anyone who tells you KM is easy is lying. KM is not for the faint of heart. It takes energy, perseverance, and an open and innovative mind to create, build, and maintain an effective KM program. KM is for the employees, not for management. Even so, one should understand that while the focus is on improving things for the workers, KM can have a huge impact on the bottom line (as we will discuss in Chapters 3 and 4).

All of our interviewees agreed that there are some fundamental things one must know, and basic tasks one must do before designing a KM program. This chapter discusses those basics.

From our interviews, we made two major observations about KM programs:

1. A vibrant living KM program produces a strong and prosperous business that proactively identifies the critical knowledge needed to adapt and quickly respond to changing business and market conditions.

2. A good KM program has two foci:

    a. Operational—where the initial ROI is often found in terms of time or cost savings.

    b. Strategic—where KM leads to business innovations and often to significant business benefits.

From an operational perspective, think of streamlining and shortening the time it takes an employee to go from newbie to journeyman and then on to subject matter expert. Now broaden your view. Knowledge sharing can take place both horizontally and vertically across organizational and geographical lines and across industries. Effective knowledge sharing within the company can be used to address business risks such as loss of expert staff, pressure from competitors, imposition of new regulatory requirements, or other unexpected market issues. Several interviewees noted that their active knowledge networks enabled their companies to react quickly to requests for proposals (RFPs) and other emergent issues.

From a strategic point of view, KM can be used to drive innovation and improve business processes. In both these arenas, a good KM program can help build, strengthen, and maintain agile organizations, thereby bettering their position and ability to continue to do well despite changing market conditions in the long term. One interviewee noted that insights gained from their KM networks has informed the strategic direction of the company by creating a new vision of what could be accomplished by better management of existing knowledge assets and planning for new ones.

Whether the KM program is operational or strategic in nature, all our interviewees agreed that the KM manager must: 1) know the driver for the KM program ("Why are we doing this to begin with?") and 2) understand the circumstances in which the KM program has to work by identifying and analyzing the stakeholders, pain points, and the current state of KM in the organization. Sounds easy, but keep reading.

KM PROGRAM DRIVERS

First, what is the KM driver? Knowing the driver or the "why" will help a practitioner frame the KM program and assist in its design. Our interviews revealed four main reasons why organizations decide to embark on a KM program. We have ranked them based on the number of programs that had that driver. In other words, of all the programs we looked at, most of them were based on risk, with the fewest number based on regulations or requirements from a higher authority. The four drivers we identified are:

1. Risk, real or anticipated
2. Desire to improve
3. Vision and innovation
4. Regulatory or higher authority requirements

Risk

Knowledge loss is often not anticipated. The risk of knowledge loss and its impact is seldom considered until it actually happens. When organizations find they have lost valuable capability, they have to play catch up and try to stop additional future knowledge loss. At Sellafield, a UK nuclear facility, management had started a KM program in response to a government management audit and were making progress when there was an unexpected offering of a voluntary separation program to the Sellafield workforce. Many long-time employees decided to leave. Faced with the unanticipated loss of more than 1000 experienced employees in a three-month period, they had to kick up the KM effort in a hurry. Sellafield decided to focus its efforts on identifying and capturing critical knowledge before it walked out the door. For Sellafield, risk had become a reality.

At the U.S. Nuclear Regulatory Commission, management decided to pursue KM when they realized that they were losing 4,000 person years of experience per year, that 50% of its staff had less than five years of experience, and that utilities had expressed intent to submit more than 20 new power plant license applications for NRC review.

The Malaysia Petroleum Management (MPM) business unit within the PETRONAS Oil and Gas Company began its KM program because other companies were "pinching" their experts, while the UK's National Health Service Digital organization, formerly the Health and Social Care Information Centre, and Lloyds Register Marine were losing experienced staff due to reorganizations and relocation. All of these organizations had risk as their primary KM driver.

Desire to Improve

Some CEOs and organizations embrace the concept of constant improvement. They see knowledge sharing, collaboration, and empowerment as a way to improve processes and streamline their business, which gives them a competitive edge. This is typically seen in organizations whose product is knowledge, organizations, such as ARUP, Digital Equipment, the U.S. Defense Acquisition University, and Deloitte. Other organizations such as Airbus, which have experienced the high cost of poor internal coordination, have "gotten religion" and are now aggressively pursuing their KM programs to improve not only their operations but also their reputations (as discussed in Chapter 4).

Vision and Innovation

Few organizations have the luxury of thinking into the future. But some, such as the Port of Antwerp, are trying new, innovative techniques to conduct business altogether. The Port of Antwerp is using adaptive case management to "work out loud" and let the workers design their own processes as they go. While there are components of wanting to improve operations, their focus is to morph into a cohesive working organization where everybody knows what their peers are doing and everyone works together to get things done.

Using more conventional tactics, the Malaysia Petroleum Management (MPM) unit within PETRONAS, the National Oil and Gas Company of Malaysia, has incorporated KM into all aspects of its business. Instead of focusing on the capability of individuals, MPM is focusing on the capability of the organization by actively encouraging employees to capture and maintain knowledge for the benefit of the organization. MPM does this while continuing to value and honor employees with reward and recognition incentives (as seen in Chapter 4). By identifying its organizational capabilities, MPM is able to examine its current knowledge needs and assets and forecast needs for the future. It has used this knowledge to inform company strategy for the next three years.

Regulatory or Higher Authority Requirements

Sellafield's initial driver for creating a KM program was an independent audit by the UK Nuclear Decommissioning Authority in 2008 that evaluated Sellafield's processes for managing and sharing knowledge. The audit started the KM ball rolling and, as noted above, KM efforts really shifted into high gear when more than 1000 people decided to take advantage of the voluntary severance package. This caused Sellafield to focus its efforts on capturing critical knowledge before it walked out the door.

Although development oriented research organizations like the International Center for Tropical Agriculture (Centro Internacional de Agricultura Tropical, or CIAT) constantly think about better ways to share information, a 2005 initiative of the Consultative Group for International Agricultural Research (CGIAR) caused all of its research centers, including CIAT, to identify key opportunities for knowledge sharing.

At this writing, a regulatory requirement to have a KM program was unheard of, but with the recent work by the International Organization for Standardization (ISO), this may change for those seeking ISO certification, and soon. ISO has convened people around the world to create ISO standards for KM that will be included in future ISO certification requirements. Hopefully these ISO standards will have sufficient flexibility to permit a breadth of KM programs and tactics that can change as situations change. No matter what people say, each company is unique with its own individual cultures and needs.

Whatever the driver, KM must support the business mission and goals and be well aligned with the organization's culture. If KM does not do these things, it will be hard to get management support and, more importantly, it will be a challenge to keep KM going when budgets are cut.

PROGRAM SCOPING TASKS

Regardless of the driver(s), all our interviewees agreed that the KM manager must scope out the "minefield" before designing the program and developing tactics for implementation. This scoping consists of three main tasks:

1. Identify and understand the stakeholders.

2. Identify and prioritize the pain points.

3. Define a baseline and metrics.

TASK 1: Identify and Understand the Stakeholders

This first task sounds simple, but most people do not spend enough time on this task. You need to look at all of the people who will benefit from the sharing of knowledge along both vertical and horizontal organizational lines. Some may even be outside these known lines and external to the organization.

How many times have you heard "I didn't get the information in time" or "I didn't know we had that information"? Business literature is filled with stories about how the ineffective sharing of information resulted in increased costs, or worse, employee injury or death. Company surveys are fine, but you learn more by talking to people. People are more open in person, and there are nuances one can glean from face to face (F2F) conversation and by observing people's body language. You will get a lot more from talking to people than any survey can provide.

In the old days, one could get the pulse of the organization and uncover production issues by spending time in the smoking lounge or chatting to people at the water cooler. The source of information is less important than the validity. Patricia gathered insights by listening to people talking about work while standing in the cafeteria lines—one of the few remaining places where people are in an informal setting and speak freely.

Do not rely on management opinion, hearsay, or rumor to identify issues. All too often these opinions and rumors are acted on in haste when actions should really be based on ground truth. Those who generate and actually use the information are better able to tell you how best to improve the flow, use, and validity of that information—again, something one cannot get from a company survey.

When you talk to your stakeholders, remain impartial and listen carefully. Ask probing questions: Who generates the information? Who transmits or shares the information? Who uses it? Does everyone who could use the data have access to it? How does the information flow within and outside the organization, and how does it affect overall productivity? Is there someone outside the organization who uses the data that we want to include? Don't stop when someone says, "we send the information to X." How reliable and effective is that information transfer? How do you know the information is needed and useful? Are we taking the data because we have always done it this way? Is there a better way to gather and share this information? Are we giving them the information they actually need?

Knowledge Maps

One technique that some find useful is knowledge mapping. The information gathered through stakeholder interviews and engagement is shown in a "map" or visual tool for documenting what knowledge is located where within an organization. When developing a knowledge map it is important to consider all potential sources of knowledge for the organization being mapped. We present some suggestions of where to look in Figure 1.

The knowledge map is developed by surveying, assessing, and then documenting how information, knowledge, competencies, and proficiencies within an organization relate to each other. It illustrates or "maps" how knowledge flows throughout an organization. Good knowledge maps can enable organizations to:

- discover the location, ownership, value, and use of knowledge artifacts,
- learn the roles and expertise of people,
- identify constraints to the flow of knowledge, and
- highlight opportunities to leverage existing knowledge.

The map can be used to show a given process, identify what knowledge is used in that process, and describe how that knowledge flows through that process. Multiple maps can help identify areas where similar knowledge is used in multiple processes. If done well, knowledge maps can show who or which group has what knowledge, where the knowledge resides, how the knowledge is transferred or disseminated, and areas of knowledge vulnerability.

Because knowledge maps characterize the knowledge held within the organization, they can also be used to make a case for addressing knowledge vulnerabilities or for preserving key assets.

Creating and maintaining a knowledge map can take a lot of time and effort in that the work of an entire group must be analyzed and documented. This often is done by convening the members of the group and then asking them to describe how they work and

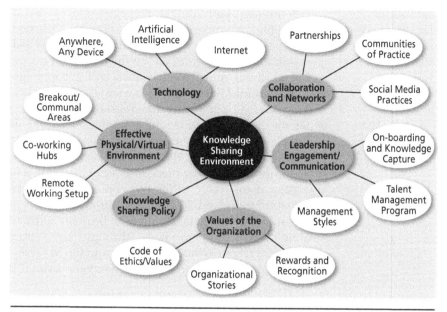

Figure 1 Map of information sources for compiling a knowledge map.
(Created by P. Corney)

the knowledge they use. A facilitator listens to the group and creates a draft knowledge map. The group is then reconvened and asked to validate or revise the map before finalizing it. The vast majority of our interviewees did not use a knowledge map; however, those who did recommended them highly.

Task 2: Identify and Prioritize the Pain Points

As you get to know your stakeholders, pain points will emerge. Management pain points may vary across departments and usually differ from those of the workers. As you talk with more and more people, some commonalities will reveal themselves. Some pain points will be related. Almost always, pain points can be addressed by more effective and efficient transfer or sharing of knowledge across organizational silos. You will undoubtedly come across skeptics who think that KM is a waste of time and just another management fad. Use them as an asset. If you can address their concerns, show them the value of KM, and turn them around, we promise that they will become your strongest ally.

"Make sure you align with the business strategy. Don't rush. People are wary about KM."

N. MOSS, LLOYDS REGISTER MARINE (LRM)

Identifying pain points is never ending. So at some point, stop and evaluate what you have learned. Which pain points can you resolve quickly? Which ones will increase productivity? Which ones do people complain about most? Which ones will get management's attention? Sometimes it is a small issue, such as making sure all administrative assistants have access to all the pertinent managers' calendars. It could be as simple as posting real-time monthly data in one place so all departments that need the data can see the same information in one place instead of emailing and resending it to twelve different people whenever the information is revised. Maybe it is editing a document online and allowing small changes to be made without sending the document back through the entire concurrence chain. Whatever it is, your first KM targets should show business process improvement, even if it is small.

The most resistance will most likely come from middle management. They are responsible for holding the company together, maintaining employee productivity, and making everything work while meeting constant requests from upper management—some of which do not seem to make sense. They also are removed from the actual work so may not know what it is currently like in the trenches. They are pulled in all directions. They, in particular, need to know "What's in it for me (WIIFM)?

One of our interviewees suggests using the SCARF® model to strategize how best to approach middle managers and to reduce resistance to KM (see Figure 2). SCARF was first published in 2008 in the *NeuroLeadership Journal.* The acronym SCARF stands for status, certainty, autonomy, relatedness, and fairness. By consciously addressing the SCARF factors ahead of time, one can reduce resistance from middle managers by addressing their fears up front, calming their worries, and showing them how KM can improve their status, provide more certainty and autonomy, and enhance their relationships with their peers in an equitable way. Winning middle managers over will help sustain the KM program when times get tough and it is well worth the effort.

What's In It For Me?

Status
Certainty
Autonomy
Relatedness
Fairness

Figure 2
The SCARF model.

Task 3: Define a Baseline and Metrics

Our interviewees noted that defining a baseline and setting up metrics in the beginning is key. It is also often very difficult to do. In a few cases, such as the NRC, saved time was easily turned into a monetary equivalent since the cost for NRC staff time is a matter of public record. For the U.S. Army, knowledge sharing was linked to lives saved. At Cadbury Schweppes, using expert knowledge to eliminate sloppy licorice translated into less lost product, which had an associated cost savings, and later to increased profit due to increased production. But in most cases, identifying a monetary metric will be difficult.

Not knowing what your metric will be, and understanding that metrics can change over time, the best thing to do at the outset is to gather anecdotal data. How long does the process take from beginning to end? How long does it take to issue a response or product? How long does it take to get information from person A to person B? Where are the bottlenecks? What do people think about a given process? Are people frustrated? How frustrated are they? Does the right information get to the right people when it needs to be there? How many complaints, either internal or external, have been made about a given process or communication? After the KM tactic has been implemented and the processes are streamlined, you can ask the same questions again and get qualitative feedback on the difference that KM made. With a little luck, perhaps the changes can be monetized later. Two of our interviewees noted that they wished they had gathered initial anecdotal data, even if only from a few employees.

It is often said that "what you can measure you can manage." It should probably be said that "what your organization measures, it will value and allocate resources to." Translating time saved, streamlined business processes, and improved decision making into terms that management can understand—a monetary equivalent—is difficult, but it is well worth the thought and effort to do so.

All of our interviewees reported the most effective "metric" as the story or testimonial. At NRC, inspectors in different regions of the country who encountered unique situations typically had to wait for in-person regional conferences to discuss and share information with their peers in the field. If the proposed solution required technical analysis from headquarters, it could take up to a year to decide whether a given technical fix was acceptable or not. After creation of an online secure community of practice, inspectors could communicate with each other and their technical experts in headquarters in near real time; the average issue resolution time dropped from months to days. Inspectors felt that their needs were identified and addressed and headquarters staff knew they were always in the loop. Morale went up and the time for resolution went down.

There is a lot of power in story. Use it.

KM is not one size fits all. A successful program considers the organization; its business strategies; management and staff expectations; organizational cultures, both in headquarters and in field offices; and the national culture in which they live and operate. That is why the three tasks are so important. If you have already started your KM program, you can still do these tasks and modify your program as needed. If your program is beginning to flounder, doing these tasks might help revive it.

SUMMARY

In this chapter, we identified four main drivers for creating and maintaining a KM program:

1. Risk, real or anticipated
2. Desire to improve
3. Vision and innovation
4. Required by regulation or other higher authority

Our interviewees were unanimous in identifying three tasks that must be done before embarking on a KM program. We discussed ways to do these tasks and identified task pitfalls, citing examples and references that might be helpful. The tasks are:

1. Identify and understand the stakeholders.

2. Identify and prioritize the pain points.

3. Define a baseline and metrics.

The next chapter will look at how to locate the mines and start crossing the minefield—getting started.

3

Entering the Minefield

If you have done the three tasks described in Chapter 2, you have spoken with a lot of people, you have a clear understanding of the organization's mission, you know where the pain points are, and you know who your supporters and critics are.

Now you need to think about how to enroll people as supporters for the KM program and prepare to counter the naysayers on why KM is not needed. Think about change management as you develop your KM tactics and develop a communications plan.

GEARING UP

If you don't have a clear enthusiastic supporter, it could be that the driver for your KM program is either risk or regulatory requirements. Even so, you must find and cultivate a KM champion. The champion need not be in the "C" suite, but it helps. In some cases you may have to cultivate the enthusiasm of your internal sponsor by telling them the various benefits they will personally gain by supporting KM. Remember the SCARF model mentioned earlier. Success can bring more visibility, increased productivity, or a reputation for successfully managing a vital corporate program.

Several of our interviewees also suggest finding an external mentor. If you do so, it is important that you find someone who is experienced in KM. Finding an external mentor or advisor can be tricky. There are many people out there who say they have KM experience, but look at their experience carefully. Did they build the program and stay with it long enough to realize a real benefit? Do they have the battle scars to prove it? Or are they just trying to get a contract or job with you? Patricia found several good mentors through her attendance at a number of KM conferences. She sought out people who had actually run a KM program for an extended length of time, and who were willing to discuss their successes, failures, and challenges. Several of these mentors invited her to see their KM program in action at their companies, invitations she readily accepted.

"There is nothing better to leverage than an ego."
A. SHELLEY, FORMERLY OF CADBURY SCHWEPPES (CS)

All of our interviewees noted that stories of success and failure can go a long way in convincing managers that KM is a good idea. Managers often look for something that can put them in a positive light. That is something to consider when developing your 'elevator speech' on the benefits of KM.

KM can be both pushed from the bottom where the staff would benefit from KM tactics and pulled from the top where managers can look good if their units are more efficient. But what about the middle levels? People in those positions often feel squeezed. They are wary of any new initiative that could upset the status quo and divert staff time from "doing work." It is very important to show them how KM will improve their group operations and possibly their personal status within the organization. When you speak to mid-level managers about KM, present KM as an asset, not a threat to their position or department. Remember and apply the SCARF method mentioned earlier.

*"Know thy
user for they
are not you."*

P. ENG

Many things can thwart your efforts before you even start, so before you take your first step into the minefield you must be clear on exactly what you are trying to do. Rather than "making things more efficient," you need to identify a real issue. Try to narrow it down to something specific that can be done fairly quickly, such as creating a common discussion space for people in different locations who do the same job, or documenting how information flows among groups so all can see the process steps, or creating a topic-based blog for people to share information at their convenience, or maintaining the latest set of online documents for a work group. Try not to impose your thoughts or management's thoughts on what might work. Remember that you are working for the workers and the work unit's interests and benefit. It is important that you focus on making *their* processes better.

KM is for those who create, use, and disseminate the information. Staff members who generate and use information at the working level are the masters at what they do and most likely have the best ideas of how to make things even better. Your job is to make their jobs easier and make sure that the KM initiative also supports the organization's mission and goals. If it saves the organization time and/or money, even better.

When you look at the pain points, look for problems that are caused by impediments in sharing knowledge, obstacles to learning from other company departments, or barriers in transferring lessons learned or best practices from one area to another. Your first pilot project should address one of these issues.

Once you have selected your target KM issue, it is important that you are able to articulate the need for the initiative, the anticipated benefit after the initiative is implemented, and how addressing that issue supports the organization's mission. You must be clear on this before you look for a technical solution.

While the information technology (IT) department can very helpful, most of our interviewees noted that IT was often quick to propose technical solutions that, when examined, usually did not address stakeholder needs. In most cases, proposed solutions consisted of new or modified software. While IT may have the technical expertise to run and maintain the software for an organization, IT usually does not understand the information needs of specific parts of the organization, how information should flow within them, and how that information is used. This is why talking to stakeholders is so important. You must understand what the work unit needs; software may not be the right answer.

Several interviewees said they felt as if the IT department thought the organization was there to support the IT department instead of IT supporting the organization. One interviewee noted that their IT department deals with "users," not customers, and did not seem to understand that IT is a support organization. Others said that their IT department seemed to treat customer requests as a nuisance rather than a business need and often dismissed or delayed responses to requests.

Not all IT departments are like this, but as the KM program manager, you must make sure that it is all about the stakeholders, not about the technical solution. With luck, you can partner with your IT department to develop the KM tools as appropriate.

When searching for solutions, try modifying existing tools instead of buying a whole new software package. As you may know, buying, certifying, and launching new software can take years depending on how onerous the software approval process is in your organization. Some KMers have encountered a lot of resistance from IT, and the effort and cost to procure new software can divert precious energy from solving the issue at hand. Several interviewees found that their existing software had capabilities that the IT department hadn't enabled because they weren't viewed as helpful or necessary. Once those capabilities were enabled, they were able to address multiple work unit needs with the existing software and minimal effort. Check to see whether your existing software can support better information sharing or creation of communities of practice. Does your existing software have a capability that your IT department has not enabled? If this is the case, you may need management support to get IT to turn that feature "on." It will help if you can present a sound business case for why you need this feature.

Change is difficult and scary to some. For those of you who remember the transition from phone calls and paper memos to email, do you recall that it wasn't until people were forced to use email that they actually embraced it? Do you remember when you first started using your mobile phone to read and respond to emails? What about texts for business? There was resistance, but texting was quick, easy, and convenient and it enabled people to answer questions from anywhere most anytime. What began as a novelty became standard practice. If you create a new communications vehicle, think about how to get people to use it. It must be quick and easy to use and streamline communications.

Patricia recalls that managers were reluctant to use a community of practice (CoP) to share information until the NRC executive who was also the KM program sponsor posted important time-sensitive documents in the CoP. He also conducted business and policy discussions in the CoP, forcing people to use it. Everyone got the same information at the same time and the managers could not blame their email for not receiving information. Figure 3 shows a version of one of the CoP created at NRC.

"When you do something by email, not everyone knows, but if you do it in a community, everyone sees it...so people do no wrong (in the CoP)."

J. GARCIA,
DEFENSE
ACQUISITION
UNIVERSITY
(DAU)

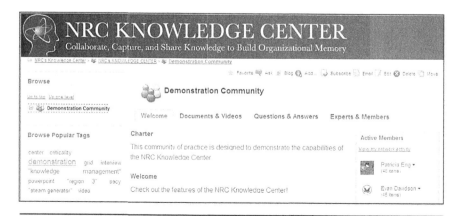

Figure 3 Example of a CoP created at NRC.

"Companies spend lots of money and time with their financial divisions, IT departments, and human resources, yet none of these pre-existing organizations are asked to define their ROI. Why not?"

G. VALA WEBB, FORMERLY OF THE ONTARIO WORKPLACE SAFETY AND INSURANCE BOARD (WSIB)

"CEOs have a short attention span."

S. GARFIELD, FORMERLY OF HP AND DELOITTE

Beware when someone tells you that they want to know what the possible return on investment (ROI) is for KM. Companies already have large departments for which no ROI is defined (e.g., administrative corporate departments such as finance, human resources, and IT). None of us have seen any calculation of an ROI for a new email or phone system, or for most software upgrades. Even so, these departments and initiatives are seen as necessary for the organization. KM also falls into that category but few realize it. If asked for an ROI you could cite the stories in Chapters 3 and 4 as examples of ROI in other companies.

Today's CEOs are focused on what happens during their tenure. In several cases discussed in Chapter 5, KM was working very well and had saved the organization a lot in operating costs. Then a new CEO arrived or a merger occurred. In these cases, the first thing that typically happens is to cut expenses. Absent a solid, ingrained belief in KM and a plethora of success stories that include savings in operating costs and/or increases in revenue, KM is usually one of the first things to be cut. It is up to the KM staff to constantly demonstrate KM's worth. Publicize success stories and the savings they bring and keep that message in front of management. If done well, it can make a huge difference in whether KM succeeds and continues or not.

Even if you cannot determine a clear monetary value for a given process, you can at least get a baseline on how long it takes to do something by talking to people about how they feel about a given process before implementing a KM tactic. You can also ask people outside the organization what they think about the process and document this "baseline." You may also wish to ask your skeptics and critics what they think about a given process. You cannot get a baseline after you start, but obtaining this information from the pertinent stakeholders both before and after KM implementation should provide you with stories and testimonials that you can use to demonstrate KM program effectiveness.

There is no substitute for talking to people, no matter what others say. Ask people what they think and what they would suggest to streamline a process or make a communication more efficient or useful. You will probably get some tidbits that you can use to help make your KM initiative an effective one.

As you design your initiatives, remember to think about how you will publicize your efforts and successes. Patricia did not develop a communications plan in advance, so when her efforts bore fruit, she did not have a plan in place to inform management that she had saved more than 37 million dollars in operating costs in the first full year of the KM program. She also did not have a plan in place to let the employees know about the various KM tools that were available to them, so the tools were not widely used. Don't make Patricia's mistake. Think about how and when you will spread the word about KM successes ahead of time so you will be ready.

TAKING THE FIRST STEP

"You cannot eat an elephant whole...you have to do it like everything else, one bite at a time."

P. ENG

So the pressure is on, you have done your homework, and you are ready to start crossing the minefield. Don't rush. Take slow small steps until you get the lay of the land. You don't have to launch an entire KM program to begin with—quite the contrary. We suggest you try a pilot project. Choose something that addresses a pain point, can be done quickly, and won't cost a lot. Managers are typically busy managing and are most likely not familiar with what it actually takes to get a job done. Ask the people who do the work to help you develop the solution. This may involve streamlining interfaces with other groups or just creating some sort of community of practice (CoP). Make sure that you listen to all of the people involved. Don't get caught up in one person's view. We cannot overemphasize the importance of talking to people and listening very carefully in order to create a good solution. Involve the workers in designing the solution and get their feedback as the initiative is implemented. You may need to tweak things as time goes on. That is normal and shows that you are open to stakeholder feedback. After all the solution is for the workers doing the job, not for you or for their managers.

Once you have a successful initiative, develop an 'elevator speech,' 15- to 30-second story that you can use to explain how a KM initiative has improved a process. This elevator speech will enable you to tell a manager from the "C" suite or other senior manager how KM has made something better when you run into them during a chance encounter. Better still if you can tell them how it impacts their specific business area. Your KM success may be something to put into the company newsletter. Whatever tactic you choose, the goal is to create a buzz that something in the company is getting better. Focus on identifying pain points and fixing them. Eventually, your efforts will be noticed and people will want to get on the KM bandwagon.

Once you have one success, pick another pain point and figure out how you can address that. Your first success story should help convince others to give KM a try. Patricia noted at NRC that within two months of her first success, people heard about it through the grapevine and started coming to her to ask questions. Some just asked questions and went away, but others wanted to learn more about what she could do to streamline their work processes, and some started CoPs. People are always looking for ways to make things easier, particularly if someone else is willing to help them do it.

These are general guidelines. Every organization is different and each one has unique challenges. We cannot anticipate what your specific needs are, so the rest of this chapter contains stories and examples from our interviewees showing where they have used KM to streamline processes. We hope that one or more of these vignettes will help you in your efforts. As you read through these stories, think about how you can use KM tactics to reduce costs and improve productivity where you are.

STORIES FROM OUR INTERVIEWEES

"Give people better knowledge, not better access to existing knowledge."

N. MILTON, FORMERLY OF BRITISH PETROLEUM (BP)

If you are starting out or are having difficulty getting management support, having KM stories to tell may be helpful. In the paragraphs below, we share stories from our interviewees that show how KM can affect organizational operations. Some demonstrate the risk one takes by not sharing information while others highlight how KM can improve company efficiency. In some cases KM tactics led to new contracts and increased revenue. Feel free to tell these stories and use them to build support for KM in your organization.

NASA and the Heat Shield

One example of where critical knowledge was not captured is the heat shield for NASA's Orion spacecraft. During her career, Patricia was assigned to work at NASA to assist in development of a nuclear powered rocket for deep space exploration. Coming from the document-centric nuclear industry, Patricia was astounded to find that NASA did not have a centralized document repository. Formal reports could be found; but some technical assessments, technical reports, and material evaluations lived on individual computers with little to no indexing or means to search and locate this information. When an individual left NASA, there was no formal standardized process to identify or capture key documents. Hard drives were simply wiped and the computers assigned to another individual. This meant that in some cases critical knowledge and communications were lost, and solutions to problems sometimes had to be reinvented at an increased cost.

NASA lost the capability to put humans in space with the retirement of the Space Shuttle in 2011 and lost the capability to launch heavy loads with the termination of the Saturn rocket program in 1973. The U.S. now relies on Russia's Soyuz spacecraft to ferry supplies to the International Space Station.

To restore U.S. capability to put humans in space, NASA embarked on the Orion project. The Orion spacecraft relies on an ablative heat shield to safely bring astronauts back from space. Ablative heat shields are designed to vaporize and burn up during re-entry to absorb the heat as the spacecraft re-enters the atmosphere, thereby protecting the astronauts. See Figure 4. Sadly, details regarding the materials and production of the heat shield used during the Apollo program could not readily be found. According to the U.S. Government Accountability Office, "the Orion project originally intended to use the heat shield from the Apollo program as a fall-back technology for the Orion thermal protection system, but was unable to recreate the Apollo material."[1]

Absent detailed design documents, NASA went to the Smithsonian to dissect an Apollo heat shield to see whether they could reverse engineer the heat shield for the Orion program.[2] This effort was not successful. In the end, NASA decided to use a material similar to the Apollo heat shield but faced a lot of testing, manufacturing, and environmental issues before they could actually use the material. No one talks about the schedule delays or cost increases

Figure 4 Heat shield protecting astronauts in re-entry.
(Credit: NASA, https://www.nasa.gov/content/five-things-we-ll-learn-from-orion-s-first-flight-test)

[1] http://www.gao.gov/assets/680/676179.pdf
[2] http://gizmodo.com/5061151/nasa-uncrates-apollo-heat-shield-after-35-years-describes-the-experience-as-a-nerd-christmas)

associated with redeveloping the heat shield. The first test of the new heat shield was finally conducted in 2014 and redesigns are still in progress. The first manned launch originally planned for 2015 is now tentatively scheduled for 2023.

NASA now pays more attention to KM, assigning that function to the Academy of Program and Project and Engineering Leadership (APPEL), which provides training to NASA employees focusing on project management and systems engineering. At this writing the chief knowledge officer had retired with no named replacement.

Identifying and Saving Critical Knowledge

"Be prepared to get out of your comfort zone."

H. MULLINDER, SELLAFIELD

Sellafield's initial driver for creating a KM program was based on a 2008 independent audit by the Nuclear Decommissioning Authority to evaluate existing company processes for managing and sharing knowledge. Sellafield Ltd.'s KM program began in earnest in 2009 and incorporated a number of business areas including leadership and cultural change, tools and infrastructure, and training, support and guidance. Shell's retention of critical knowledge (ROCK) program is considered by many to be the gold standard for corporate knowledge capture and retention and served as the inspiration for Sellafield's KM program.

The subsequent announcement of a voluntary severance program (VSP) led to an immediate, prioritized focus on retaining critical knowledge before it walked out of the door. KM efforts shifted into high gear.

"This initiative was all about the people. You need to help and support them in getting out of their comfort zone."

H. MULLINDER, SELLAFIELD

Following the VSP announcement Sellafield implemented a phased release program over a three-month period for those employees who were leaving the company. Given the tight time constraints, the KM team developed a prioritization method for selecting those employees whose knowledge would be captured or transferred. The assessment criteria considered the value of the individual's knowledge to the business, whether there were staff who would serve as new custodians for specific knowledge, and whether the new custodians were willing and available to take part in a series of knowledge capture and transfer activities. If there was no "customer" for the knowledge, it didn't make sense to capture it. Knowledge customers included peers, new graduates, and staff in other functional areas in the organization that either used or relied on that person's knowledge.

Specifically Sellafield decided that:

1. If there was no "customer" for the knowledge, it wouldn't be captured.

2. Knowledge capture sessions would focus on the needs of the knowledge recipients.

The Sellafield KM team created a three-tier system to identify and capture critical knowledge: Bronze, Silver, and Gold.

- Bronze: where local knowledge capture and transfer arrangements were already in place and had been endorsed by the line manager and recipients.

- Silver: where a KM facilitator would support the expert through several interactive group sessions. Sessions could be semi-structured interviews, concept mapping, or a group question-and-answer event. Knowledge customers attended all sessions to make sure that their information needs were met.

- Gold: Same as Silver candidates, but sessions were videotaped.

"Most people don't know what they know because it is so ingrained."

H. MULLINDER, SELLAFIELD

For all Silver and Gold candidates, the KM team held face-to-face meetings with subject matter experts (SMEs) and their managers to ensure that all were aware of and comfortable with the level of effort and the nature of the knowledge capture activities. During the capture and transfer sessions, facilitators guided the SMEs through the process and drafted a map of their knowledge, ensuring that technical terminology and acronyms were clearly explained. Knowledge customers asked questions and facilitators confirmed that each knowledge area was fully covered before moving on to another area.

After the sessions and interviews, the KM team validated results with the experts to make sure that the captured information was correct. The SMEs and knowledge customers also communicated after the sessions on their own to ensure that session documentation was accurate and current, and met together informally to discuss the topic further as needed.

Sellafield noted that two major principles were fundamental to their KM approach:

1. It is best to use multiple methods to address explicit, implicit, and tacit knowledge capture.

2. It is a mistake to store captured knowledge in a stand-alone repository. Better to make the new, enhanced knowledge available in places where the user will actually look for it.

By using their prioritization process and the three-tiered approach, Sellafield optimized the effectiveness of their KM team in a time-constrained situation. Once the crisis passed, the KM team continued to apply their experience to proactively identify persons whose knowledge needed to be captured before a staffing change takes place. Absent a crisis and time pressure, Sellafield can work with the SME and potential knowledge customers to consolidate explicit knowledge, capture implicit knowledge, and transfer tacit knowledge. Sellafield continues its comprehensive knowledge capture program to this day.

Resolving Inspection Concerns

Often, information is not shared widely enough or in a timely manner to permit optimal use of that information. At the U.S. Nuclear Regulatory Commission, field inspectors located across the country were tasked with inspecting compensatory security measures at more than 100 U.S. nuclear power plants following 9/11. New security requirements were issued shortly after 9/11 with little detailed guidance as to what was and what was not acceptable. Each utility took a slightly different approach to meeting the new requirements. NRC inspectors were tasked with assessing plant modifications and determining whether these modifications met the new security requirements. There was no common information repository or communications vehicle for inspectors to share information in a timely manner. Because the requirements were new, inspectors had to consult with headquarters staff to evaluate the acceptability of a given modification. Inspectors worried about consistency. Specifically, they were concerned that a given modification would be deemed acceptable at one plant but not at another. Because the inspectors were located across four time zones, getting a definitive response from headquarters could take some time. Under the KM program, a secure, closed community was set up just for the inspectors and the headquarters evaluation staff so they could share information on what modifications were acceptable and why. This allowed inspectors and evaluators to discuss specific modifications in near real time. As a result, the time needed to evaluate and either accept or reject the security modifications was reduced from months to days.

Capture First—Sort Later

For a variety of reasons, the Intellectual Property Office of Singapore was faced with losing approximately 30% of its staff in a two-month period. Their KM staff interviewed department managers to identify the knowledge they needed to retain. Managers were asked to identify what knowledge had already been captured, who owned the pertinent documents, and what had already been archived. Armed with that information, and pressed for time, KM staff went through the email of the staff that were leaving. They flagged those emails that were relevant and those they thought might be of value and then archived them for future sorting. With so little time and few KM staff, their approach was capture first, sort later. For those staff who clearly had critical or historical knowledge, such as a 30-year veteran, open sharing sessions were held to facilitate the capturing and sharing of knowledge. After the mass exodus was over, KM staff spent the next two years working with management to go through the archived emails, establish a taxonomy, and identify which knowledge should be kept and which could be discarded.

Creating and Supporting Communities of Practice

The Defense Acquisition University (DAU) is part of the United States Department of Defense. DAU's mission is to provide certification training to the defense workforce on requirements and processes for the acquisition of goods and services to support U.S. military operations. While DAU provides certification training for acquisition and procurement activities, each branch of the military actually certifies its own staff.

DAU takes a holistic approach in its efforts by providing certification training, continuous learning tools and opportunities, mission assistance, and 24/7 online job support. Online resources include communities of practice (CoPs) and DAU's online encyclopedia of common defense acquisition topics: ACQuipedia.

"A CoP is just another resource for the acquisition workforce."
J. GARCIA, DAU

Communities of practice enable the acquisition workforce to collaborate and share acquisition information and know-how wherever and whenever they need to. DAU created and maintains the CoP platform and facilitates a number of communities on acquisition topics for various aspects of acquisition such as program management, contracting, and logistics. When creating a new CoP, DAU engages stakeholders across all branches of the military, DoD, and others as appropriate. Once the key stakeholders are identified, DAU facilitates a face-to-face (F2F) workshop where attendees are asked to identify and prioritize their challenges, issues, and pain points.

"The community allows practitioners to share what they know; including lessons learned…and also allows CoP members to benefit from the sharing."
J. GARCIA, DAU

As is often the case with new CoPs, attendees are initially reluctant to spend time at the workshop but soon realize that they have much more in common than they had first thought. They can actually help each other. In this way, DAU creates a CoP core group up front with stakeholder buy-in on what issues to address and in what order. DAU continues to create new CoPs as needed and continues to support existing CoPs.

DAU also established and maintains ACQuipedia, an online encyclopedia of common defense acquisition topics, and provides links to the relevant policies, regulations, guidance, tools, best practices, and available training courses for a given topic.

ACQuipedia serves as a ready resource for busy acquisition professionals who need to quickly come up to speed on a variety of topics associated with the often complex acquisition process. (See Figure 5.)

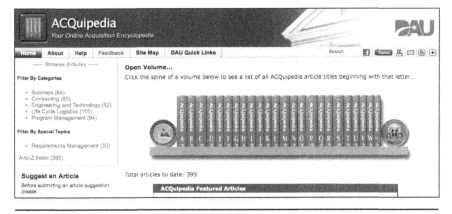

Figure 5   ACQuipedia: DAU's online encyclopedia of common defense acquisition topics. *(Courtesy of DAU.)*

DAU has also provided additional KM support by developing and maintaining a CoP implementation guide on how to establish and manage a CoP. This guide contains helpful hints on how to set up a CoP and suggestions on how to manage them. It was used by the U.S. NRC when setting up their CoPs. The guide is online at: https://acc.dau.mil/CommunityBrowser.aspx?id=170879.

Empowering Personal Assistants

The KM manager at Cadbury set up a CoP for the personal assistants (PAs) assigned to Cadbury senior executives around the world. Many of the PAs did not know each other, but the community gave the PAs their own place where they could share information on how to do things for their bosses. Before the CoP, each task would be done on the fly as needed, sometimes reinventing the wheel. Now with a place to share information, PAs could do things more efficiently. For example, how do you set up and run a conference? For years, each PA would start from the beginning, often reinventing the process each time. KM staff set up a standard spreadsheet that identified things that needed to be done, offered a suggested timeline, and provided data on how much a conference might cost. The PAs also shared information on good places to stay or eat for a given destination and how to get a visa for a given country. As a result of their collaboration, personal assistants were able to get things done in less time, with more consistency and less frustration.

Deleting Regulatory Requirements

"Before you delete something, make sure you understand why it was put there in the first place."

P. ENG

During Patricia's career with the NRC, she came across a case where a facility operating license required measurement of a certain quantity on a periodic basis to demonstrate that a required safety feature was working properly. Over the years, different engineers at the facility had been placed in charge of the surveillance test procedure and the procedure had been revised several times for various reasons. One day, Patricia watched plant staff conduct this test and noted that they were not measuring the quantity called out in the facility license. After some investigation, she found that several years before, a young engineer had decided that measuring the quantity was not necessary and that a qualitative observation was sufficient. He had revised the procedure to delete measuring the quantity. The change to the procedure had been reviewed and approved by the entire technical management chain as being appropriate. Since the plant was not measuring something that was required by the operating license, it was in violation of its operating license. NRC issued a significant safety finding and issued a civil penalty—the first ever received by that facility—in the amount of $250,000. That number is small by today's standards, but at the time, the negative press and increased NRC scrutiny of the facility was a big deal. The facility has since been shut down and is in the process of being decommissioned.

Changing Horses In Mid-Stream

Lloyd's Register has been involved with knowledge management consultancy work since 2003 and appointed a full-time KM professional in 2006. Lloyd's Register focused on developing and delivering knowledge retention and transfer (KRT) services targeting knowledge loss due to retirement and the potential loss of critical expertise. Within Lloyd's Register Marine, the KM Program grew to five people by 2008.

In 2011, the KM team was working to embed KRT process into the organization when Lloyd's Register Marine announced the relocation of its headquarters from London to Southampton. As is often the case with headquarters moves, many of the employees indicated that they would not move to Southampton. Lloyd's Register Marine faced the possibility of losing most of their experienced senior staff with the upcoming move and realized that their new KRT process could help them capture this expertise before it walked out the door.

"Make sure you clearly align with the business strategy."

N. MOSS, LRM

The KM team reshaped its KRT process to meet the new need and to embed it into the HR processes associated with the relocation. To address the potential loss of expert knowledge, Lloyd's Register Marine developed a business continuity plan that asked managers to identify business-critical knowledge and the individuals who had that knowledge. The KM team then used a KRT framework that consisted of four stages:

1. Complete a knowledge capture survey: an online survey provided to all individuals impacted by the move to identify critical knowledge, key contacts, resources, and lessons learned.

2. Create/review the knowledge portfolio: a summary of the survey results given to the individual respondents before forwarding to management for consideration.

3. KRT work: face-to-face interviews with specific individuals identified by management to develop mind maps for specific areas of expertise.

4. Knowledge sharing plan: develop and implement knowledge transfer methods appropriate to the given circumstance. This ranged from transferring files from an individual's computer to a group drive, or facilitating turnover meetings between the expert and potential successors, to developing training courses in a business-critical area.

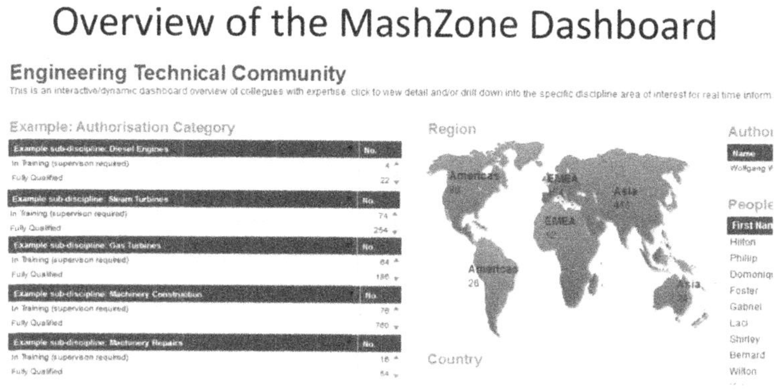

Overview of the MashZone Dashboard

Engineering Technical Community
This is an interactive/dynamic dashboard overview of colleagues with expertise. click to view detail and/or drill down into the specific discipline area of interest for real time inform

Figure 6 Overview of the Lloyd's MashZone Dashboard.
(Reproduced with permission from Lloyd's Register.)

"Start small, prove your point, show how you add value, and then scale up."

N. MOSS, LRM

In the beginning some experts were hesitant to participate in the KRT activities. "Word of mouth" was the most important tool for getting buy-in from these experts and it played a large role in bolstering the credibility of the knowledge transfer work. By the latter stages of the KRT project in 2014, individuals were approaching the KM team offering their help and asking to take part in additional KRT work. The insight gained from the KRT work also enabled the KM team to later gather dispersed information into a useful interactive online dashboard to identify the location of company expertise and knowledge assets to forecast future areas of knowledge risk (see Figure 6 above).

Using KM to Save Lives

Communities of practice (CoPs) can save lives. The U.S. Army used CoPs not only to share information but also to save lives. On their return to base, U.S. patrols in Iraq were debriefed and asked to identify one or two highlights and/or changes in enemy tactics. KM staff set up CoPs, called unit networks, specifically for these patrol leaders, using their input to design it. In one example, the enemy had begun a practice of booby-trapping posters of Saddam Hussein in Iraq so that when someone tried to remove the poster, it would explode and kill or wound the persons trying to remove it. By the day after the first occurrence, everyone knew to check the poster before removing it because the information had been put into the CoP and patrol leaders had read about it before going on patrol (see Figure 7). When the enemy changed how the improvised explosive device (IED) attached to the poster was activated (i.e., moving the location of the detonator), that change was also captured and communicated the same day across the entire company.

The Army also created an innovative training tool entitled Leader Challenge. Using video, leaders are invited to share incidents that challenged their skill set. The videos are broken into two segments. The first segment presents the problem but with no solution. Trainees view the first segment through the online training community and are asked what they would do in that situation. After submitting their answer, trainees are able to see and compare the responses of other trainees. After these two steps are completed, the trainee sees the second segment, which reveals what actually happened. The Army has found this to be a very effective training tool for new leaders.

Figure 7 Soldiers removing a poster of Saddam Hussein in Iraq.

The Leader Challenge tool became a centerpiece for community learning and the development of expertise. Many of the segments were selected for training leaders using a more robust story line. In these larger vignettes, leaders are put into the critical moment of decision and then asked to analyze the situation and identify their options. These "think like a Commander" exercises provided leaders with the opportunity to vet their proposed solutions with both peers and experts to learn how to think things through rather than just react.

Making More Candy for the World

In the mid-2000s, Cadbury introduced a center-filled gum candy—a liquid center surrounded by chewing gum and finished with a hard candy coating. When it was first introduced, fifteen factories around the world were working at full capacity in order to meet consumer demand.

The global KM manager persistently badgered people from the center-filled gum factories around the globe to get together on a 30-minute conference call. He knew that people in different countries had experienced different problems making the center-filled gum and he was sure that once they got together, the discussions would take off. Although they protested, the KM manager was insistent and after all it was only 30 minutes.... So they reluctantly agreed to get together. He was right. Once the candy makers started talking to each other, they realized that they had much to share. Thirty minutes was too short.

That first phone call showed the candy makers that there was a lot of knowledge scattered around the world within the company, and that knowledge could be leveraged to make a real difference. They realized the value of collaboration and knowledge sharing, and demanded not only more conference calls, but a website and a CoP. Eventually, some of the candy makers met F2F and figured out how to increase their global capacity by 20% by just tweaking the process.

Consistent Decision Making Saves Operating Costs

In the Canadian public sector insurance industry, the key decision making role, the one where the most risk resides, is the person deciding whether or not to accept a claim. If the insurance company does not pay out, they run the risk of being appealed. The Ontario Worker Safety and Insurance Board (WSIB) is a public sector organization and more open to scrutiny than most. Therefore there is a political cost associated with not paying out on claims too often or with paying out inconsistently. Management was worried about potential legal issues associated with making wrong or inconsistent decisions regarding whether or not to accept a given claim.

The KM staff worked with the operations staff on the set of decisions needed to determine the amount of the payout for an accepted claim. A given individual in operations might have to make this kind of decision once a month, but across the company, the decision was being made thousands of times in a given year. KM created a decision support tool that restructured the information needed to decide how much to pay. The tool identified four sub-decisions, supplied a decision map, and included the resources needed to make each of those decisions. This enabled staff to use company-wide knowledge on what constituted an appropriate pay-out in a consistent manner. The tool was successful and the leader of operations directed managers to make sure that all staff knew about and used the decision tool. As a result, claims decisions were made more consistently, more quickly and, most importantly, more accurately across the organization.

Sloppy Licorice

For 20 years, Cadbury had a problem with getting its licorice candy to set reliably. Licorice is made by combining the ingredients at 140 degrees and then turning the liquid out into a pan where it is supposed to set into a solid. Strangely, from time to time, the licorice didn't set and the frequency of it not setting appeared to be random. When licorice doesn't set, the whole batch is a loss and has to be thrown away; overall production goes down. A young microbiologist determined that in the early part of the harvest season, sugar cane has a higher proportion of starch to sugar, so the sugar industry uses a heat-stable enzyme to extract more sugar from the early harvest sugar cane. One of the ingredients for licorice is molasses, which is the syrup obtained from raw sugar during the refining process. Depending on when the molasses was made, the heat stable enzyme would be present. When the molasses containing the enzyme was added to the licorice mix, it would break down the starch in the flour such that the candy would not set. It was "sloppy."

The fix was simple. The microbiologist revised the licorice-making procedures to require testing for the enzyme and not using the molasses if the enzyme was present. The "sloppy licorice" phenomenon stopped and production became more reliable.

Everything was fine until the factory was moved to another location. Although the manufacturing equipment made the move successfully, not all of the procedures did. Managers thought they had been making licorice successfully for years, so what could be simpler? Within a year the sloppy licorice problem returned.

None of the managers had any idea of how to solve the problem, but a factory floor worker remembered that they had resolved the problem some years before. A month-long search throughout the company's online network found the microbiologist who had originally identified the enzyme working on a different continent in a different area. He told them how to solve the problem, the procedures were revised to include the enzyme check, and the sloppy licorice problem went away again.

Simplifying Institutional Documents

Starting in 2009, the International Center for Tropical Agriculture (CIAT) developed an innovative way of using blogs to involve stakeholders in the project implementation process. Across CIAT the researchers are encouraged to blog about their work and their findings throughout the year. These blogs are very active and the leadership recognizes and acknowledges their value. Blog posts are considered in the production of the annual report and CIAT annual reports are very short; they provide a short summary of research results and contain links to blog posts and other relevant information. Blog entries may also be used for project reports. This use of blog entries makes periodic reporting much easier and quicker.

We hope that these stories have given you some ideas of how to begin crossing your minefield. Your first initiative doesn't have to be large. It doesn't have to be expensive, but it does have to make people's jobs easier and support the organization's mission and goals.

As KM starts to take hold, be careful to remain objective. A little success can be seductive. Are you still listening to what people say they need? Are all the right stakeholders involved? What do your critics say now? Is there something to be learned from their comments? Do you need to update your elevator speech? How does the initiative fit into the organization's strategy? Yesterday's success is old news. Highlight your new ones.

SUMMARY

In this chapter we identified things you should do in the initial stages of staring a KM program:

- Find a champion.
- Choose a pain point and develop a pilot project that is quick and easy to implement.
- Make sure you understand the problem you are trying to solve.
- Figure out what needs to be done and get stakeholder input before looking into technology solutions.
- Modify existing tools if possible before searching for new ones.

- Get a baseline before addressing the pain point.

- Develop an elevator speech and update it frequently to highlight and publicize your successes.

- Don't rest on your laurels—look for the next problem to solve.

We also provided a number of KM examples from our interviewees in the hopes they might stimulate some creative thinking on KM initiatives or serve as stories you can use to encourage KM in your organization.

4

Keeping KM Going—
When It Is Working

You might be a year or so along your KM journey, or you may have been at it for a couple of years. Either way, it is probable that you either have or will encounter "land mines" that can damage the credibility of the KM program and lead to reduced support and the possible demise of your KM journey. Perhaps the initial burst of enthusiasm for KM has worn off, your sponsors have turned their attention elsewhere, you have a new sponsor who thinks that KM is running itself and doesn't need any attention or energy, or your company is going through a merger or acquisition and the new administration doesn't see the value in KM so is proposing to cut the program. KM is like that: people start to take it for granted when it's working because it is transparent to them. They have no idea how much is going on behind the scenes, how much thought has been put into these KM tactics, and how these tactics support the organization.

In this chapter we will look at what it feels like when KM is really working in the hopes that these examples and stories will help you when you encounter your own land mines.

PROVEN SUCCESSFUL KM TACTICS

KM: Evolving From Blogs to Informing Proposals

The International Centre for Tropical Agriculture (Centro Internacional de Agricultura Tropical, or CIAT) is an international non-government research organization that covers the tropical areas of Latin America, Africa, and Asia. It works to reduce hunger and poverty and improve human nutrition in these areas through research focused on increasing the eco-efficiency of agriculture (see Figure 8).

One of fifteen specialized research centers of the Consultative Group on International Agricultural Research (CGIAR), CIAT employs about 1,000 staff globally and is funded by a multi-donor CGIAR Fund

Figure 8 Collecting water samples, Tana River Watershed, Kenya. *(Reproduced courtesy of CIAT. Credit: Georgina Smith/CIAT)*

as well as by grants from many organizations, some of which are also fund donors. One of CIAT's KM challenges is to capture knowledge and lessons learned from their research projects and build that knowledge into the process of developing grant proposals.

CIAT has worked hard to improve knowledge sharing, online collaboration, and embedding KM into research activities by building institutional knowledge. CIAT has an open access policy and makes this knowledge available horizontally across the research community.

A few years ago, CIAT adopted a results-based management (RBM) framework as a way of designing projects with a focus on results, their expected use and project impact.

As noted in Chapter 3, CIAT encourages researchers to blog about their work and report on their findings throughout the year. This has proven successful in that if a researcher has been blogging all year long, writing the annual report for that project is easier. Both donors and funders are eager to see how their money has been spent and blogs help keep people informed.

Projects require periodic meetings with the various research partners but travel budgets are normally one of the first items to be cut when money is tight, so virtual meeting tools are being used more and more. Recognizing that knowledge sharing is key, CIAT is working to expand and develop its KM team skills regarding the design and facilitation of collaborative processes for face-to-face and virtual interactions both within the organization and with its research partners.

CIAT continues to work on improving its agriculture data repositories as well as its data management practices and tools for researcher use. Specifically, CIAT is looking now at using insights gleaned from blogs, from other knowledge-sharing activities from the past, and from existing projects to improve the writing of grant and funding proposals by asking "where can I find what we already know?" and "who do we know who has already done it?"

Innovative Ways of Implementing KM

During a long KM career that spanned some major US corporations (Digital, Compaq, HP, and Deloitte), one of our interviewees has seen a lot of KM initiatives. He shared some of them with us as well as his observations about KM in general.

"Get your leaders to do the thing they want everyone else to do."

S. GARFIELD, FORMERLY OF HP AND DELOITTE

One of the big challenges KM managers face is to get people with influence to do the things that will have the most impact. In the mid-2000s Hewlett Packard's (HP's) printing business was the largest profit center within HP. The senior vice president for that business realized that he needed to think about the long term. Specifically, what could they do to improve their already successful printer business and maintain their market share in the future? Rather than have a management retreat with selected managers, he started a blog, made it open to every employee in the business, and asked them for their thoughts and opinions. It took a while but people started to provide input and the senior VP personally responded to each and every post and comment. His direct and personal involvement not only energized the business, it generated employee loyalty and resulted in more managers creating and using blogs to communicate with staff.

"Focus on things that work really well and celebrate those times."

S. GARFIELD, FORMERLY OF HP AND DELOITTE

As is the case with large geographically distributed companies, organizational silos developed within HP. Something needed to be done to stimulate knowledge sharing. KM staff assigned points to various KM activities, such as posting something in a discussion board, commenting on a blog post, leading a CoP, and so on. At the end of the month the top point earners were recognized and asked to write up their stories, which were then published in the company newsletter. As the program progressed, winners received monetary awards that clearly demonstrated that the company was committed to and valued KM.

Leveraging Community

During the course of his career, the young micro-biologist mentioned in Chapter 3 worked in the area of quality and continuous process improvement. Through this he learned that people on the production line were masters with unique manufacturing insights that could and should be shared across the business. He later became the global KM program manager for Cadbury. We previously discussed the center-filled gum community and how the attendees, initially reluctant, came to appreciate sharing knowledge in the community. But that is not where the story ends.

"KM facilitated conversations that influenced those with the budgets."

A. SHELLEY

In the beginning, the managers for the center-filled gum factories around the world were too busy being busy. The center-filled gum was made in fifteen factories around the world with global sales of $100 million per year. Cadbury wanted to make more product and decided to build a new factory in the U.K. It was going to take two years to build the factory at a cost of tens of millions of dollars with only a projected 5%–10% increase in global capacity. The KM manager convinced the production line managers to gather on a 30-minute conference call in which they realized the value of collaboration. These calls continued and problems that had arisen in one country helped those who encountered it in another country. The line managers demanded more and longer conference calls and convinced their management to pay for these calls and give them the time to attend them.

After several discussions, a number of the factory managers decided to get together at the factory in Turkey and try tweaking the production line. This meant stopping production for Cadbury's most profitable confection for a few days. Despite corporate push back, the factory managers stood firm. Their efforts paid off; their tweaks resulted in a 20% increase in production capacity with no capital investment. The UK factory was no longer needed to increase production. That increase in production translated into a revenue increase of 20 million dollars per year—more than the 5%–10% that the new factory would have produced, and without a substantial capital investment Clearly a case where getting the people who actually do the work together was worth the time, effort, and expense.

From Tape Recorder and Pen to Sustainable Corporate KM Program

Shell's (see Figure 9) Retention of Critical Knowledge (ROCK) program has long been considered by many to be the gold standard of corporate knowledge capture and retention. It has been going strong for over a decade and served as the inspiration for Sellafield's KM program. ROCK began with a structured interview process captured with a tape recorder, paper, and pen. It was originally set up to capture knowledge from retirees to meet the challenge of 'the big crew change,' the anticipated loss of a majority of experienced petroleum industry staff projected to occur in 2013–2014. The issue was less of a workforce retention issue and more of an organizational capability issue.

ROCK began with just a tape recorder, pen, and paper, and consists of a structured interview process with a trained facilitator. Participation in ROCK is voluntary and there are no formal incentives to participate. Candidates are selected according to their perceived knowledge, so being asked to participate is considered an honor. Senior managers often sit in on the interviews. The interviewee's successor and peers attend the interview as do others with a vested interest in the topic. The biggest value is in the interactive sessions where subtleties and nuances can be drawn out and explored. As always, the biggest challenge is time. The interview process can take up to 12 hours to complete.

ROCK started in 2005. ROCK Lite, targeted at people transferring jobs, was created in 2006 and ROCK X, created in 2007, targets experienced hires. Knowledge captured from the ROCK interviews is used as a sort of reference book with information used in relevant CoPs, lunch-and-learn sessions, and, where appropriate, in the Shell online encyclopaedia that contains Shell-specific information organized by topic.

But ROCK is not Shell's only KM tool. Shell encourages employee participation in their topic-based Shell international global network (SIGN). SIGN provides a global on-line community and professional

Figure 9 Royal Dutch Shell logo.

network within Shell. There is also an internal expertise finder to help locate experienced colleagues to help solve emerging problems. These tools help Shell keep 92,000 employees connected around the globe.

Shell's KM program has stood the test of time and some of the team have been working in KM for over two decades. Managers have KM goals in their job descriptions and are assessed against these goals during their annual appraisals. KM is embedded across the business and is included in the learning curriculum, reflecting the close relationship between the two areas. It is a comprehensive program and has served as the inspiration for a number of KM programs.

WHEN KM IS WORKING

KMers often struggle to convince senior management that KM has real value. Even so, occasionally a statistic or story comes up that goes a long way toward changing management perceptions. Almost universally, our interviewees acknowledged that, with hindsight, they would have spent more time on metrics, stakeholder and management engagement, and making sure they always had an elevator speech ready to demonstrate the value of KM, preferably in terms of increased productivity and saved costs. We present stories from our interviewees that demonstrate what can be done when KM is really working.

Solving Problems Without an Office

From its creation, Arup has embedded good principles of knowledge management (or sharing) into their working practices. Arup's core values were first articulated by its founder, Ove Arup, and are articulated in 'The Key Speech' of 1970. Every Arup employee is given a copy of 'The Key Speech' to read. Collaboration and agility are emphasized throughout the organization, company expectations about sharing and participation in forums and networks is strongly encouraged, and personal development, which includes knowledge sharing and performance, is included in performance appraisals. Arup reinforces the importance of knowledge sharing through its skills networks, skill-focused communities of practice that connect people using face-to-face (F2F) initiatives, online networks, and discussion forums. These skills networks facilitate knowledge sharing and collaboration and also link practitioners to each other, enabling the sharing of information quickly anywhere in the world. More than half of Arup is subscribed to more than two skills networks and a quarter of Arup is subscribed to four or more networks.

In 2012 Hurricane Sandy hit New York City, flooding both the subway system and all the tunnels connecting Manhattan to the mainland (see Figure 10). Arup's New York office was inaccessible. An Arup principal asked the global skills network about subway and tunnel flooding solutions to support a client request for a white paper and presentation with graphics on specific subway system and tunnel flooding precaution solutions for the next day. Responses came in quickly from around the world, enabling the Arup team to deliver the white paper and presentation even without a functioning office. The presentation was sent to the Metropolitan Transportation Authority chairman and Arup was invited to do a feasibility study, develop long-term flood mitigation plans, and provide technical construction support for eight subway stations across Manhattan.

Figure 10 Flooding in the New York City subway.

At Arup, knowledge sharing and transfer is about connecting people to deliver innovation. Where there is an improved way of operating, they actively seek to embed it into their processes. They work hard to raise awareness of best practices throughout the organization. Every year each skills network contributes to a skills network statement. These skills network statements provide an overview of all the skills networks and their activities and provide Arup executives and the Arup University Council with an understanding of how the skills networks are functioning and developing. It also informs skill leaders across Arup on what other skills networks are doing. This sharing of perspectives on 'what good looks like' creates opportunities to learn from one another. Arup's commitment to KM is unmistakable in that is it embedded in its corporate culture and enables Arup to make the most of best practices and expertise located around the globe.

Improving Design and Manufacturing Processes

Every aircraft manufacturer fears delivery delays because of the impact on both revenue and reputation. In 2000, Airbus decided to build the largest passenger airplane ever built, the A380. Major structural sections of the A380 are built in France, Germany, Spain, and the United Kingdom. The sections are then transported to Toulouse, France, for assembly. Shortly after the A380's maiden voyage, Airbus announced a six-month delay for initial delivery. A year later, Airbus announced another six-month delay. Investigation revealed that the delay was due to electrical wiring issues resulting from the use of different versions of the software design tools used by the French and German designers. Airbus took steps to remedy this situation before delivering their airplanes, and this caused the delivery delays.

"We want to collect learning points from people who worked on the previous project."
R. OGHOUBIAN, CIMPA

In order to avoid future delays and to improve its overall design and manufacturing processes, Airbus took a radical approach when designing their next aircraft, the A350. They would aggressively use KM techniques to identify lessons learned and pursue best practices by engaging the designers and manufacturing staff who worked on the A380 with the intent of streamlining the design and manufacture of the A350. The goal was to optimize the design, minimize unplanned maintenance without compromising safety, and avoid the mistakes made with the A380.

Airbus identified their subject matter experts and interviewed them to capture critical knowledge and identify things that contributed to the difficulty in building the A380. It then convened a company-wide lessons-learned effort consisting of a number of F2F workshops attended by the people who worked on the A380. Managers insisted that their staff attend workshops in person and Airbus flew employees from their home countries to Toulouse to insure their attendance. The workshops were time consuming, averaging a full day in length. It was called the 'Big Peer Assist.'

"It wasn't only learning from lessons learned, it was also about learning from good practices… and the third leg of the stool is the questions or employee needs."
R. OGHOUBIAN, CIMPA

The workshops were facilitated by KM staff and the attendees were asked three questions:

1. What worked well that you would want to repeat?

2. What did not work well and what would you not want to repeat?

3. How can we improve the manufacturing process?

The issues raised at the workshops were combined with aircraft maintenance histories from the existing fleet and tracked using an Excel spreadsheet. Airbus Aircraft Architects vetted and dispositioned each issue into one of four categories:

1. We know about this and the fix is included in the design.
2. We don't know about this; we will examine and inform.
3. We don't know where to find the solution and may seek external assistance.
4. This is something we cannot fix now, so it is a risk that we will have to mitigate.

Employees were encouraged to bring up things they wished they had been able to do during the initial design and manufacture of the A380, things they were unable to do because of schedule pressure. Some items resulted in new and innovative design changes, some changed how the plane was fabricated, and some decreased assembly time, but all were thoroughly vetted by a multi-national workforce that was highly motivated. In the end, Airbus delivered a very mature A350 design for certification and has set the standard for future airplane design (see Figure 11).

Figure 11 Airbus A350.
(Credit: Airbus)

Knowledge for Delivery

The United Kingdom's National Health Service (UKNHS) is always under scrutiny. Following the merger of two organizations within the UKNHS, a new CEO arrived at the Health and Social Care Information Centre (HSCIC), now NHS Digital (NHSD). The new CEO and his new executive management team (EMT) created key performance indicators (KPIs) to measure organizational effectiveness. The EMT director who volunteered to take on the KM KPIs did so because of his experience working on the London Olympics. Impressed with the presentation from the KM team lead, he authorized expansion of the KM team.

Once established, the KM staff created a process for gathering, reviewing, and implementing staff recommendations for improving operations. They called it Knowledge for Delivery (K4D). At the end of a project or task, employees were invited to conduct a lessons learned exercise, but instead of calling them "lessons learned," the KM staff called them recommendations for improving future efforts. They found that using the phrase "improving future efforts" generated more participation in the meetings than in previous "lessons learned" meetings. It implies that something will actually be done with the recommendations. The KM team provided guidelines and facilitation support for these exercises, all the while emphasizing the importance of improving future efforts.

K4D has become a widely used recommendations management tool where anyone in the business can propose ideas to improve any NHS Digital processes. Once a recommendation is written, it is submitted through the KM portal and evaluated by a central review panel (CRP). Panel members review the recommendation and decide whether to implement it. If requested, KM staff assist employees in writing the recommendation, which has to address the following:

- What happened that brought about the learning?
- What was the impact?
- Why did it happen?
- What do you recommend others do in order to repeat your success or to avoid failure?

The people who submit the recommendations and the subject matter experts in that area are invited to discuss their recommendations with the central review panel online for several weeks. At the end of the discussion period, the group meets to decide whether or not to implement the recommendation and develops action items as appropriate. Everyone involved can track the status of a given recommendation and follow its progress throughout the entire process.

K4D is very effective. Although the previous lessons learned process might result in a change, it would often take a year or more of discussion and multiple reviews. Some K4D action items have been implemented in as little as two months because all the decision makers were involved in the discussion from the beginning.

"How do you want us to support you?"

S. LAYTON, NATIONAL HEALTH SERVICE DIGITAL (NHSD)

Early on, the KM lead asked the volunteer KM champions scattered throughout NHSD what sort of support they wanted and needed and held a K4D exercise to open the discussion. The champions responded that they wanted an online discussion venue and to meet in person quarterly. There is nothing like face-to-face discussions. Agendas for the quarterly meetings include an update on KM within NHSD, a call for issues and solutions, and a mini training session on topics not normally available through the training department such as business writing. The meetings are so enjoyable that the KM lead has frequently had to increase the size of the room because more and more people were coming and were getting things done.

"No one should be having that much fun at work."

S. LAYTON, NHSD

For one of these quarterly meetings, attendees were asked ahead of time to pick any problem that needed solving. The overwhelming favorite issue was that meeting rooms were poorly soundproofed. At the meeting, attendees used the K4D process to develop potential solutions. Some were very creative, such as attaching thick rugs to meeting room walls. They had so much fun trying to solve the problem that they got complaints from the meeting room next door. Attendees in that room told them that they were having too much fun.

Celebrating and Rewarding KM Contributions

When KM is working, people at all levels are engaged and success is celebrated and rewarded. However, what one culture considers a reward others might consider a punishment. In the United States, a designated parking space might be considered a great incentive for getting involved and producing exemplar performance; in Europe or Asia it might not be a motivator at all. There is no "one size fits all" in designing incentives. Again, it depends on the organization and its culture.

"(There is) critical knowledge that all staff in the whole division needs to attain. That is transformed into the Knowledge Book—online courseware—and is kept current."

A. ISMAIL,
MALAYSIA
PETROLEUM
MANAGEMENT
(MPM)

Malaysia Petroleum Management (MPM) is a business unit within the Petroliam Nasional Berhad (PETRONAS), the national oil and gas company of Malaysia. MPM plays the dual roles of resource owner and contractor manager by managing hydrocarbon assets in Malaysia. They began their KM program with a bottom-up approach in 2003. MPM was not immune to losing good people, some of whom went to their competitors. KM groups were set up in each department, asked to capture critical knowledge, help fill knowledge gaps, and manage the MPM enterprise-wide "institutional capability" initiative with the goal of creating company capability as opposed to maintaining knowledge in specific individuals.

To do this, MPM began by creating knowledge maps to identify existing knowledge assets and knowledge needs for all departments. This effort is not a trivial one. The initial knowledge mapping exercise takes a full day and involves roughly 5% of the experienced staff. After the initial event, more time is spent going back and forth between the staff and the KM team to make sure that the maps are accurate. The whole process takes about a month and produces a map that identifies the critical knowledge, who has it, and who uses it. The map can also point out areas of knowledge risk where there are only one or two people with a particular knowledge. If those people are near retirement, the risk may be higher still. The final maps are shared with management and are reviewed annually to ensure that a knowledge map for a given department remains current. In 2015, MPM produced more than 200 knowledge maps for 8 departments in 13 areas.

By knowledge mapping departments, KM staff can identify what knowledge is used or needed on a daily basis, what critical knowledge needs to be captured, and how to forecast future knowledge needs. Management can then identify organizational strengths and vulnerabilities and see how the workforce aligns with the overall business strategy.

Figure 12
MPM Expresso logo.

MPM also uses CoPs, discussion forums, and an in-house tool called the Expert Experience Sharing Session, EXPRESSO for short (Figure 12), to capture critical knowledge from SMEs. The EXPRESSO interviews vary in format and include one-on-one meetings, small-group meetings, and sessions in front of an audience. Interviews are videotaped and edited down into segments, tagged, and uploaded to the KM portal. Knowledge from the EXPRESSO interviews that management decides all employees should know is then compiled into an online knowledge book and made available to all staff. Employees are required to go through the knowledge book and are given both a pre-test and post-test to determine whether they have learned the information and to identify any knowledge gaps. In this way MPM ensures that all employees have a consistent understanding of management-designated topics and information.

*"People have
to be able
to replicate
learning or
success in the
next project and
be more effective
or efficient."*

M. SHARIFF,
MPM

Groups within MPM showcase their KM activities through the annual success story competition. Individuals and groups are encouraged to share their project achievements or failures and show how KM was or could have been used to either achieve success or avoid failure. The goal is to highlight KM tactics, share stories, and determine whether KM tactics would be useful elsewhere in MPM. KM staff note that if not for this company-wide competition, many successful KM tactics might not come to light. In 2015, more than 700 stories were submitted. Success story winners are invited to a meeting with senior executives and the annual award ceremony is attended by the PETRONAS top management.

MPM has also created a KM loyalty scheme allowing employees to earn points by participating in KM activities such as contributing to a CoP, attending an EXPRESSO session, and so on. The points transfer onto a PETRONAS loyalty card that can be used to buy merchandise or fuel at any PETRONAS petrol station in Malaysia. Individual KM performance also counts toward the overall departmental KM performance, which is also recognized at the annual award ceremony.

MPM KM staff note that employees don't talk in terms of knowledge sharing; they talk in terms of EXPRESSO. In 2015, PETRONAS saw a 60% increase in participation in the EXPRESSO program and a 10% gain in knowledge re-use from the success stories presented in previous years.

The MPM program goes a long way to address the "what's in it for me?" question many KM programs fail to tackle. They have identified the importance of recognition and rewards in terms of tangible and visible personal outcomes such as awarding loyalty points and giving monetary prizes that are directly related to an individual's participation in knowledge sharing and transfer. Up until recently, the KM program was managed in individual businesses and operating units. In April 2016, KM was centralized and elevated to serve all of PETRONAS as a single corporate entity. This KM program is definitely working.

SUMMARY

In this chapter we provided instances where KM program managers implemented a variety of KM tactics and initiatives with very positive results. We also provided examples where KM programs were working in the hopes that these stories will inspire or assist you in building your own successful KM program. Real KMers share. Feel free to use any of the tactics described here.

5
Killing KM

Something that few people talk about is the decline and demise of a successful KM program. Toward the end of Patricia's tenure at NRC, management priorities shifted away from KM. No one said to stop doing KM; they just didn't encourage people to stay involved. KM participation slowly declined. In doing the interviews for this book, we found that other programs had suffered similar fates. In all the cases we looked at, KM program decline could be attributed to a change of management and/or a withdrawal of executive support, often following a merger or acquisition. Several of our interviewees ran very successful company-wide KM programs for several years, but in the case of Digital Equipment, BP, and the U.S. NRC, these programs either fizzled out, became more localized, or essentially went on hiatus. We felt that it was important to examine these programs to help you avoid a similar fate.

THE NRC STORY

Despite the fact that the NRC KM program was run by a single individual with no budget or staff, it was widely recognized throughout the U.S. government as a highly functioning KM program saving the NRC more than 37 million dollars in operating costs in its first full year of implementation. At that time, the KM champion was the second highest executive in the agency. Committed to KM, he would repeatedly mention KM in meetings and in informal discussions with managers. Often he would ask senior executives how their specific KM initiatives were going, frequently in senior staff meetings. Senior managers from each office were expected to attend a quarterly KM steering committee meeting and designated departmental staff were expected to attend monthly working level KM meetings.

There was a flourishing knowledge center that consisted of electronic communities of practice, and the NRC held an agency-wide half day Knowledge Fair to showcase agency KM initiatives. The Fair was attended by over 50% of the staff, even though it was only four hours long. A year later, NRC received the 2010 MeriTalk Merit Award for its efforts in streamlining government.

"It is nonsense to say that KM is running itself or that it should be embedded in the work itself. We don't say HR or Finance is running itself."
S. GARFIELD, FORMERLY OF HP AND DELOITTE

Everything was going smoothly. Then management changes occurred that would adversely impact NRC's KM program. First, the KM function was moved from the executive director's office (the "C" suite) to Human Resources reporting to the training director. The training director had recently joined the NRC from another agency. He was not familiar with either NRC's mission or the information needs of the staff. A long-time training manager, he viewed KM as a sort of hybrid training program. He knew it was doing well but thought that NRC could use a training course on what KM was. His first order was for staff to develop that training course, possibly buying it from someone else. Since the budget for KM now fell under training, funds used to support NRC's knowledge center were slowly reallocated to non-KM training courses and tools. Next, the executive KM champion was transferred and the oversight for KM given to another executive who believed that KM was running itself. Although he did nothing to detract from KM, he did not actively support it either. Managers were no longer questioned about their KM activities and "C" suite interest in KM waned.

Absent proactive and vocal support from the "C" suite, management attention to KM decreased and senior managers stopped attending the steering committee meetings, instead sending mid-level managers who were not familiar with the KM program and who viewed the meetings as time away from the "real work." Decisions stalled and soon the departmental staff stopped going to the monthly KM meetings altogether, saying that they had too much work and could not afford the time to attend.

Having run NRC's KM program single-handedly for four years with no budget or staff and now with little to no management support, Patricia was exhausted and retired from NRC. Since KM was not seen as a priority, she was not replaced for over a year.

THE BRITISH PETROLEUM STORY

BP embarked on a comprehensive KM program in the 1990s. At that time they were focused on building collaboration and removing silos. They surveyed others who were pursuing KM at the time and set up a KM organization. The KM staff toured the business units worldwide, asking them to identify their business issues, and listened carefully for those where the inability to share knowledge or to learn from each other were the root cause. They then ran small-scale trials in 1997 and presented proposed pilot programs to the steering committee in 1998 with implementation scheduled for 1999. The 1998 pilots delivered more than 100 million dollars of value, which was accounted for in the 1999 budget requests. The plan was to create more than 100 KM managers who were embedded in the business units in order to create KM assurance standards for BP and monitor KM effectiveness against those standards.

Then in August 1998, BP merged with Amoco. The typical aftermath of any merger or the arrival of a new CEO is aggressive cost-cutting and this was no exception. As previously noted, new post-merger CEOs do not stay with their new firms very long—just long enough to cut costs, show increased profits for a year or two, and then leave before the cuts wear away those profits. As is often the case in mergers, no one from the Amoco team knew what KM was, let alone understood the 100 million in savings that BP had previously enjoyed. Without warning, the technology budget that included KM was cut by 50% in mid-year. The KM staff left the company, leaving BP without a corporate KM program.

THE HP/COMPAQ/DIGITAL STORY

"In corporate think, KM is not viewed as one of the functions corporations have."

S. GARFIELD, FORMERLY OF HP AND DELOITTE

The KM program for Digital Equipment was started in 1996 to support knowledge sharing and collaboration across engineering, service, and sales. Information flowed quickly and enabled Digital to respond quickly to customer issues and concerns. KM was strongly supported by Digital management. In 1998, Compaq Computer bought Digital Equipment. There was some interest in KM and the program continued. Information continued to flow. In 2002, Hewlett Packard (HP) merged with Compaq. The former Digital Equipment KM program manager eventually took over HP's worldwide KM program and implemented social networking before all of HP's competitors. They then instituted a KM point system where staff could earn points by their participation in a community of practice: asking a question, answering a question, uploading a document, and so on. The process was automated and there was a leader board to foster competition. In 2005, HP got a new CEO who focused on cutting costs, but KM was part of the consulting organization and continued to hold its own. Then in 2008 HP bought EDS and major cost-cutting followed. The entire consulting business that contained KM was abolished. The KM program manager who had worked in KM for decades and built a vibrant KM program now found that his KM services were no longer necessary. He left HP two years later.

Can one prepare for these "land mines?" Yes and no. Each case suffered from outsiders not understanding the value of KM and the value and cost savings it brings to the organization. When the manager comes from outside the organization, if KM is to survive, a strong business case must be made in terms that the new manager can hear.

Patricia noted that despite receiving the 2010 MeriTalk Merit Award and issuing a press release about the award, NRC executives did not know that the KM program had saved NRC more than 37 million dollars in operating costs in its first year of implementation and 22 million dollars the following year. BP KM staff had been told that they had strong executive support and were very focused on their task. Following a merger, the entire program was cut without consulting anyone about KM effectiveness. The KM program originally developed at Digital Equipment survived two acquisitions and a new CEO but not a third acquisition. All of these KM programs were vibrant and successful in their day.

The loss of all of these KM programs was due to the new management's lack of awareness of the value of KM. Would a concerted publicity effort have made a difference? What about strong advocates in the top executive ranks? Could that have saved KM?

All of the interviewees who suffered the loss or deterioration of a KM program noted that they could have done a better job of touting the successes and benefits of their KM program. In retrospect, they thought that they could have been more aware of the corporate politics and taken that into account as they considered potential changes to their KM programs. If not planned for, mergers, changes of CEO, or the loss of an enthusiastic KM champion at any level in the organization will adversely impact KM. The best we can suggest is to plan for it, just in case....

"Dead, but it won't lie down."
P. CORNEY

But then again.... in one of Britain's National Health Service organizations, NHSD, KM was languishing and near death when a new CEO/executive management team (EMT) arrived on the scene. The KM program manager did her homework, learning about the EMT director's past work, his likes and dislikes. She read everything she could find about him from anywhere she could. One of the hot buttons was key performance indicators that were introduced to NHSD for the first time. She crafted a presentation highlighting how KM could help track KPIs and more, carefully designing her presentation to account for his love of cycling. As a result, she got the go ahead to increase the size of the KM team. She worked hard and was able to get her KM program back on track. It went from near death to becoming a flourishing program. Hers is one of the examples in Chapter 4 on what KM looks like when it is working.

So, there is hope after merger, but one has to be ready to adapt. Bottom line, the best you can do is to always have your stories ready to tell and your elevator speech tuned to the manager's way of thinking. Be flexible, align your efforts as closely as possible with your organization's strategies and goals, tout your successes, and be persistent.

6

What We Admired and Why

We are very grateful to all of our interviewees and appreciate their willingness to share both the good and the bad about their KM experiences. We admire their dedication, tenacity, ingenuity, and sheer bloody mindedness to do what they believed to be the right thing in the face of significant opposition. While all of the KM programs we looked at are noteworthy, we would like to highlight some things that really stood out and won our admiration in the hopes that these stories will also inspire you in your KM efforts.

Using the experience of the entire organization to improve company design and manufacturing processes.

AIRBUS

In Chapter 4 we mentioned that Airbus drew on past mistakes and successes when developing the A350 aircraft. It is much more expensive to change an aircraft design after certification, so Airbus worked hard to anticipate issues before submitting the A350 design for certification. The process that they went through to identify lessons learned from their A380 experience and improve the A350 design experience is truly noteworthy.

Airbus began the design process for the A350 airplane by asking some hard questions:

- How can we harvest the knowledge we've accumulated from past experience to develop a mature design?

- How can we use the maintenance history and data of the current fleet to improve the new design?

- What sort of KM tactics can we use to facilitate answering these questions?

As previously noted, Airbus asked its customers what they wanted in a new airplane and held company-wide workshops to get employee input and to build a sense of team across the multi-national workforce. Through these workshops they identified internal communication and design issues, and used the KM team to facilitate these meetings.

Airbus vetted every issue identified during what they called "the Big Peer Assist" using simple tools—an Excel spreadsheet—proving that one need not spend a lot on fancy software to do amazing things. But they did more than that. Airbus focused on learning from both good and bad practices and addressed the biggest obstacle head on. Realizing that there was limited sharing across both geographical and corporate boundaries, Airbus established open plan offices for each project and frequently pulled people together in face-to-face sessions, no longer relying on virtual meetings for communications.

We were amazed at the Airbus level of commitment to learn from previous projects and use those lessons to improve their processes. They really put their money where their mouths were, reconfiguring office space and flying employees to Toulouse for the Big Peer Assist.

ARUP

Making KM personal in a creative, collaborative environment that encourages and acknowledges knowledge sharing.

Ove Arup created an organization where the culture supports the sharing and transfer of knowledge across 37 offices around the world. Knowledge capture is less important than knowledge transfer. Whenever there is a potential improvement to how Arup operates, Arup seeks to capture it and feed it back into business processes. The corporate ethos is all about sharing, and the expectation is that everyone will participate in forums and networks. Employee participation in KM is also explicitly included in their annual performance appraisals.

KM at Arup tackles the "what's in it for me?" question head on by supporting personal skill development, and maintains a corporate university to underpin knowledge sharing from the top down with support at the individual level with networks, discussion forums, and communities.

We admire how Arup incorporates KM in everything it does and how the skills networks not only form the basis of the KM effort but also directly support the business.

MALAYSIA PETROLEUM MANAGEMENT

A comprehensive KM program clearly linked to business goals and strategies and the use of 'gamification' to assure employee participation.

KM began in MPM as a 'just do it,' relatively unstructured bottom-up initiative in the early part of 2003. KM is now integral to the MPM way of working and supports the overall goals of fourteen institutional areas of its business. KM content is aligned with MPM strategic goals and is used as a means to achieve those goals in that MPM focuses on preserving the capability of the company as opposed to the capability of the individual, although individuals are encouraged to share information and participate in KM activities. Involvement in KM is acknowledged and rewarded.

MPM has a well-run knowledge capture program in EXPRESSO, but uses other tools as well. They also compile critical information into a knowledge book that all employees are required to read. Pre-testing and post-testing determines whether knowledge was successfully transferred. KM is celebrated MPM-wide with an annual competition to showcase notable KM activities and an awards ceremony attended by top MPM executives. Since the interview took place, MPM's KM program team has been elevated and is now working across all of PETRONAS. We were truly impressed with the scope and breadth of the MPM KM program as well as MPM's dedication and commitment to KM.

SELLAFIELD

A great example where after addressing an unexpected loss of staff with critical knowledge, the company has embedded knowledge capture and retention in its day-to-day operations.

Shell's knowledge capture program has long had its admirers. So, using the principles of good KM and learning from what others have done, UK Sellafield decided to use Shell's ROCK framework as a start when it was faced with the loss of more than a thousand staff at the same time it was charged with implementing the recommendations from an audit by the Nuclear Decommissioning Authority (NDA).

The KM team began by asking line managers what knowledge should be captured. They then prioritized their efforts based on the value of the knowledge to the organization and whether there were customers who would use/need this knowledge.

The KM staff trained people on knowledge capture and facilitation tools, and provided interview tools aimed at getting the interviewees to continue speaking and to expand on their answers to questions.

When the mass exodus was completed, Sellafield had collected a focused body of material that they knew was needed for the organization. Most would have stopped there, but Sellafield continues to this day to identify and capture knowledge important to the organization. The bottom line is that Sellafield has embedded KM into day-to-day processes and this approach has informed the nuclear decommissioning best practice guide. We were impressed that a quickly pulled together, yet effective effort has formed the basis for Sellafield's continuing KM efforts. Most would have stopped once the initial crisis was over.

7

What Surprised Us

If there's one thing we've learned conducting the research and reflecting on our combined experience, it is this: although there are often generic similarities, most KM programs are unique in both conception and implementation. Why? To come back to an earlier theme, "it is all about the people" and each organization has its own culture and ways of working.

It wasn't a surprise to discover that organizations with the most vibrant programs were those for which knowledge is the core product or where the loss of critical knowledge can have catastrophic repercussions. Although in some cases, captured critical knowledge was still abandoned, as in the case of the NASA heat shield and the sloppy licorice.

As we looked at the various KM programs, we saw some things that we didn't expect to find in our research. In this chapter we reflect on what surprised us and why.

Though English is a common and first language, we see and hear different things in the same words.

Surprise #1

While listening to and later summarizing the interviews, Patricia and Paul saw and heard different things. Despite the fact that both of us speak English as our first language and grew up as "baby boomers," there were times where we heard very different things in the interviews. In fact, as we wrote this book, we found phrases and terms that just didn't translate between English and American and that needed explanation and clarification before we could proceed.

Both Paul and Patricia have worked with different cultures. Paul once worked with a start-up company that had persons from six nationalities, none of whom spoke the same mother tongue. All had English as a second language. It quickly became apparent that what each said was interpreted differently by the others. He used a variant of the "repeat-back communication" widely used in the U.S. military and elsewhere to streamline communications. In the beginning, during discussions where it was unclear that people understood each other, he would say, "I heard you to say and I understood you to mean," until the management team got to know each other better.

Although that worked in a small start-up, larger global decentralized organizations where English is the working language face other major challenges including culture issues and the need to convince employees to change how they do their work. In Patricia's experience, people were deeply immersed in the nuclear and scientific community, which had its own culture and jargon, so she rarely experienced these types of communication issues, but several of our interviewees who worked in companies having offices around the world did.

There are many documented instances on the web where the use of a word in one country is perfectly acceptable, but not in another. We both knew this and had no communication issues until we provided draft text to each other. Then odd words popped up in the draft requiring explanation. This rarely happened when we spoke to each other. Perhaps we are less concerned with the spoken word than the written word or perhaps we can glean meaning through conversational context. Not until things were written down was that cultural business jargon revealed. For this reason we decided to include a glossary and references in this book so that the reader has a better chance at understanding what we are trying to say. Even so, there may be things that some people will not understand.

Even in specialized areas where special language and jargon are routinely used, mistakes can be made. Two of our interviewees cited *The Checklist Manifesto* by Atul Gawande as recommended reading. In the book, the author illustrates how the use of checklists dramatically reduced the post-surgery mortality rate in hospitals around the globe. The checklists covered everything from pre-op set up and familiarization through to post-op wind down while accommodating cultural and linguistic nuances. Patricia notes that at the NRC, NASA, and the military, checklists are used extensively to address potential anomalies and minimize errors and loss of life. Even so, mistakes are sometimes made. Paul has also seen similar results with clients who have introduced knowledge-enabled checklists into standard operating procedures.

Operational KM to the fore, strategic KM to the rear.

Surprise #2

The majority of KM programs appear to be operationally focused and tend to address a burning platform issue or urgent business problem. These programs usually address knowledge risk (for example, loss of knowledge due to downsizing, retirement, reorganization, or acquisition). Some programs focus on making processes more efficient, meeting internal and external quality standards, or adhering to regulatory requirements. However, few programs that we looked at seemed to be driven strategically as a result of visionary leadership. In many cases the KM function is located within an operations division or unit (for example, research, human resources, or training). Rarely is a chief knowledge officer part of the "C" suite of an organization. Often, as is the case of CIAT, KM is moved around within the organization. Over the years, CIAT's KM team has been located in a number of different areas; at this writing the team is housed in the research part of the organization as part of program coordination. They believe that knowledge sharing and making meetings better is a support function for research activities, so it is housed there. At NRC, KM began in the "C" suite but after two years of success was moved to the training department.

The danger of being narrowly operationally driven is that when the burning platform issue or business problem gets resolved, KM is often left without a clear purpose. Programs without a clear purpose are easily cut.

We estimate that less than one KM program in five is strategically aligned; where they are, it is usually because knowledge is perceived to be the organization's core product. Companies such as Arup, and in the early days Digital, depended on employees knowing how to solve problems. Knowledge sharing across continents was important. Organizations such as PETRONAS and the Port of Antwerp have realized the importance of recording who knows what and making sure that information is shared to ensure that capabilities are maintained. Their programs are closely tied to their organization's strategies and long-term business goals.

Knowledge is not seen as an asset by many.

Surprise #3

Few people during our research mentioned knowledge as an asset or the product of a process. Everyone engaged in knowledge sharing or knowledge transfer recognized the intrinsic value in collections of audio and video material from knowledge capture interviews; however, we did not get the sense that knowledge was viewed in the same way as a tangible company asset—something to be inventoried and protected. PETRONAS is an exception in that they seek to maintain institutional capability.

One of Paul's clients tells this story:

"My wireless keyboard stopped working so I ordered a new one. It cost less than $20. Today someone from Premises comes to my office and puts a sticker on the keyboard with a barcode. He says, "It's okay now it's shown in our inventory of assets" and goes away. That same day the company's first US Patent notification arrives complete with a certificate. It cost about $30k to acquire, not to mention the time spent developing the idea. It's not shown as an asset of the organization yet its revenue potential is huge and it needs to be maintained."

If you lose your laptop, chances are you can replace it, but how difficult is it to replace the content, your knowledge? You may have backed up your machine - in that case you have managed and stored what you know, including your knowledge assets.

Although the company most likely guards its patents as intellectual property, the fact that it is a knowledge asset is transparent. We spend vast amounts developing knowledge products but often fail to record or treat them as assets. At NRC, Patricia developed a list of subject matter experts with critical knowledge that was updated annually. Too often companies don't think about maintaining them as we would a fixed physical asset. Perhaps because organizations don't produce inventories of knowledge assets they find it difficult to measure the effectiveness of a KM program.

Again, MPM/PETRONAS stands out in that it is less interested in maintaining capability in an individual and more interested in maintaining capability in the organization. This is what Patricia calls "organizational memory."

The lack of clear metrics and the importance of stories.

Surprise #4

KM has been around for more than two decades yet there still are no universally recognized standardized metrics to measure its effectiveness.

However, there are many KM measurement models that attempt to highlight and acknowledge the progress a given KM program has made: the Most Admired Knowledge Enterprises (MAKE) award; River Diagram; and KM Maturity Model to name three.

The danger with these benchmarking models is that they are subjective. Many organizations use transactional data such as number of page visits, number of CoPs, or number of comments made in a given CoP to show usage of a system or knowledge base. That doesn't mean that they are effective in sharing or transferring knowledge across the organization.

As mentioned earlier, some KMers look at how long a process took before KM and how long it took after KM. Several of our interviewees were able to point to production increases or time saved and present those changes in monetary terms (for example, increasing center-filled gum production by 20%, as discussed in Chapter 4). Although these 'wins' are often one of a kind, they can be used to show what KM tactics can do.

"...We've developed metrics but it's the qualitative examples that still have the most value..."

D. POOLE
AVERY, ARUP

We had expected to discover some 'silver bullets' regarding metrics and ROI during our research. In a way perhaps we did since many told us of their use of stories and participation in company KM competitions as one way of illustrating KM success and involvement. MPM holds annual competitions where employees "compete" by sharing stories of how they used KM tactics to make something better. MPM tracks the number of success stories they receive and how many are implemented elsewhere in the organization, but they don't keep metrics in term of money saved. Even so, the annual award event is considered a flagship event attended by senior executives and it underscores the importance of KM and acknowledges that it is all about the people.

So while there are no standardized metrics or KM statistics, measurements that work are tied to an organization's strategic goals and expressed in the terms meaningful to its management and culture.

You need to devote at least 25% of the KM resource to promotion/ engagement.

Surprise #5

We were surprised at how frequently we heard interviewees say they wished they had spent more time managing stakeholder concerns and expectations. A common theme that surfaced in our interviews was that unless you spend time and resources on engaging and communicating with your stakeholder groups, management in particular, you are going to lose your support.

People have short memories. Yesterday's success or cost saving is quickly forgotten. The focus is not on "what have you done for me in the past?" but on "what can you do for me in the future?" Most new KMers do not develop an ongoing communications and engagement plan. The first few successes are publicized, but often that outreach effort fades away. We are constantly bombarded with information in the office, during our daily commute, and at home. Can you remember the last time you heard something positive that affected you? Can you remember a KM initiative that made a difference where you work? Unless it was very recent or impacted you directly, probably not. It is much easier to focus on the negative and on how difficult something is versus how sharing information made something easier or cheaper.

"Find the highest leader with the biggest problem and fix that to get support."

A. SHELLEY

Since KM is seldom publicized, you need to bring KM successes to people's attention and remind them of what KM can do. Your outreach program doesn't have to be big, but it has to be persistent. Core components include your KM elevator pitch, a one-page schematic of the KM program that you can use when talking to people about what KM does and how it works, and a strategy to address the 'What's in it for me?' question. This last is possibly the most important issue.

One of our interviewees discussed factors to consider in stakeholder outreach and engagement and suggested using Dr. David Rock's SCARF model as a tool for analyzing and addressing stakeholder concerns. Middle managers often present the most resistance to KM because they are being pulled from both top and bottom. Staff want more freedom and less oversight, while upper management want results and

and no problems. The managers in the middle just want to do their jobs and be promoted or transferred to where they are no longer being pulled from both directions. Using the SCARF model can help one develop communication strategies to convince people that KM is not a threat or a waste of time but actually is a tool to help them look and perform better. KM is something to be supported instead of avoided. Again, SCARF stands for:

- Status: People fear that their status will be threatened.

- Certainty: People fear that KM will bring uncertainty and that their position will be threatened.

- Autonomy: People fear that they will lose control and that they won't have choices.

- Relatedness: People are unsure of how this will impact their relationship to others within the organization

- Fairness: This might or might not come into play, but some may be concerned about it. Will it be transparent?

Regardless of what model you use, think about how to engage your stakeholders at all levels and keep that awareness going. Maintaining awareness of KM effectiveness will be helpful in maintaining support for your KM program.

Surprise #6

KM is not considered in mergers or acquisition.

A number of the KM programs were driven by risk and focused on knowledge capture and retention in order to mitigate the loss of critical knowledge from people who might leave following a downsizing or move. It is interesting that during and after a merger, there is often no thought given to retaining critical knowledge. This may be because CEOs don't think about knowledge assets as company assets.

"Human capital should be one of the most important assets."

M. PREVOU,
FORMERLY
U.S. ARMY

"Unlike computer systems and tanks, KM is not tangible. People don't understand that KM has to be systemic and built-in."

M. PREVOU,
FORMERLY
U.S. ARMY

You can count the number of sustainable KM programs on one hand.

We heard of no initiative or program to identify and map critical knowledge assets that were put in place to prepare for a merger or acquisition. We also did not hear of any effort to compare unit performance before, during, or after a merger or acquisition to detect changes in knowledge assets or critical knowledge. Some of the examples in Chapter 2 pointed out the potential consequences for discarding or changing operational procedures without looking at why things are the way they are. If an organization maintains an inventory of knowledge assets and demands the same of its merger or acquisition partner, transitions might be smoother.

In a couple of examples our interviewees saw their KM programs eliminated or severely reduced post-merger because the new management regarded KM as a cost that could be saved rather than as an asset to be maintained. Interviewees who experienced this attribute the cuts to ignorance and, in part, to their failure to maintain the KM outreach efforts discussed in item 5 above.

Even in cases where KM saved organizations tens of millions of dollars, management still did not recognize KM as a valuable tool to streamline processes and increase productivity. KM has a long way to go before the "C" suite recognizes it as an important part of any integration plan after a merger or acquisition.

Surprise #7

Can you name three KM programs that have stood the test of time over five years? It's a question that's often asked by skeptic CEOs and CFOs. The answer is, "Yes I can but there aren't many." Some of these were discussed in Chapter 6, "What We Admired and Why." Others that come to mind are the World Bank and the Olympic movement. Yet if you look at the speaker rosters at KM conferences, you see many of the same names appearing every couple of years telling the story of a KM program at their new employer.

Why is that? Our best guess is that sustainable KM is a long-term bet, not a short-term fix, and that many of today's corporations and CEOs are focused on the short term, not the long term. As one of our interviewees said, "KM is not viewed as one the functions that corporations have" and another said, "KM was done in spite of management." Often the continuation of a KM program depends on the "C" suite. If they see the value and possibilities that KM can bring, the program continues. Shell, Arup and PETRONAS are good examples of where the "C" suite supports KM. Even if the KM program saves lives, there is no guarantee that it will survive. The U.S. Army KM program was severely curtailed in 2012 during the U.S. budget sequestration.

As seen in Chapter 5, even outstanding KM programs are abandoned or decline for a variety of reasons. And because there is no real career path for KMers, a KM manager who does not have another skill may find it easier to do KM at another company than to be assimilated into the company that killed its KM program.

Surprise #8

Perhaps this is not surprising. The majority of the people we spoke to have been doing KM for over a decade and started at a time when there were few, if any, accredited KM programs.

In the UK, knowledge and information management is seen as one of the professions of government with a learning curriculum in the process of establishment. Universities and business schools in both the UK and the US have knowledge and information management graduate and postgraduate courses. There are also numerous KM communities around the world attached to business schools and universities where KM practitioners gather to share experiences and work on research of mutual interest.

A few organizations offer a KM certificate, but in most cases the people who teach these courses focus on cognitive theory and business practices and examine case studies. It is rare to find someone who has actually built and lived with a KM program for any length of time who teaches KM. Most KMers either stay in the field or retire and move on to other things rather than teach.

Some corporations have created their own corporate university and in some cases include KM as part of the curriculum. Having this credential is helpful within the corporation, though it remains to be seen whether a qualification from one corporate university will be acceptable elsewhere.

Even with all the education and training programs for KM, there is no recognized industry body that has established any sort of universally agreed KM qualification or certification criteria. Instead, global KMers are attracted to training programs run by private organizations so they can demonstrate their familiarity with KM through external credentialing. While knowledge of the theory behind KM and how the mind works is helpful, real knowledge is gained through experience on the job, and there are few mentors or coaches to help new KMers take their first steps. That is, in part, why we are writing this book—to share the lessons learned from people who have actually managed a KM program and have the battle scars to prove it.

To further complicate matters, as we already noted there is no clear career path for KMers. The average life span for a KM program manager is about four years. At that point, and absent additional resources or explicit management support, one wants to do something else. Many senior KM people change roles or organizations, going to another company to build KM elsewhere. One interesting point is that KM managers who have truly done the job know and understand the relationships among the various sectors within the company. They have a unique perspective of how the organization functions and can see who is and who is not a team player, what the sticky issues are, and where communications can be improved. In companies where management is progressive, these KM managers can be a valuable asset in developing company-wide tactics and strategies for improving and streamlining operations as well as candidates for challenging assignments.

People are still more important than technology.

Surprise #9

With so many companies using forms of artificial intelligence to store, search for, and catalogue information, it was surprising to find that people are still struggling with search. For years, people have predicted that technological advances would make knowledge work easier, yet search continues to be one of the most difficult tasks people do in the workplace. The failure of new software to improve search may be an artifact of choosing the tool before understanding what the need is. While at NASA, Patricia found it more effective to use Google software outside the firewall than to use the Google search tool provided on the NASA intranet.

Although company IT departments work to improve their search engines, our interviewees noted that the best way to find something quickly was to use topic-specific communities of practice created for and maintained by employees who understand the business and who know how information is used within the organization. They can tag and highlight information using company-specific terms better than any software can.

The biggest challenge in maintaining a vibrant CoP is keeping the CoP active. People have to be interested and willing to access and use the technology. They have to see that their input and contributions are valued. As discussed in several examples in Chapter 4, much can be done to get people to participate in CoPs. Most importantly, the CoPs must be designed for and managed by the people who need and use the knowledge in them.

In the end, it is still all about the people.

There is an increasing interest in creating KM standards.

Surprise #10

As of this writing, there are few recognized standards in the West governing KM activities. But that may be changing.

Every government has an organization with auditors who evaluate how well various government agencies deliver services to the general population. In the U.S. that agency is the Government Accountability Office (GAO); in the UK it is the Government Audit Office.

Dubai has chosen to base the Dubai Government Excellence Program on the European Foundation for Quality Management (EFQM) quality standards. These standards include a section that discusses delivering effective KM. The Dubai Government Excellence Program includes clauses for use by independent assessors when assessing the performance of government bodies. Compliance with the Dubai standards results in certification, which is highly sought after in Dubai to demonstrate an acceptable level of performance. Organizations can use various means to achieve certification.

In the international locomotive industry, the International Railway Industry Standard (IRIS) calls for effective KM and asks railway and locomotive manufacturers to demonstrate that they have a KM program in place as part of their certification review. Failure to get IRIS accreditation can adversely affect a manufacturer's ability to sell locomotives.

The International Atomic Energy Agency (IAEA) describes a number of KM tactics that facilities might use in several IAEA guidance documents, but stops short of requiring a KM program. Similarly, several nuclear industry organizations have produced topical documents that discuss KM but do not require a formal KM program. Instead, these documents point out the benefits of having a KM program in place.

While there was no definitive KM requirement, the main initiator of Sellafield's KM program was an audit conducted by the UK Nuclear Decommissioning Authority to look at how knowledge was being shared at Sellafield.

The International Organization for Standardization (ISO) is currently working on KM standards with an expected publication date in 2018. Paul is a member of the British Standards Institute (BSI) KM Standards Committee working on the draft ISO standard. Publication of these standards has the potential to increase industry interest in KM; however, given the uniqueness of each KM program, creating definitive requirements and metrics for determining program effectiveness will be difficult.

Even though there seems to be a move to create standards for having a KM program in place, there are no guarantees that a company with certification will have a KM program anything like another company that is also certified. These standards can only define a minimum common denominator, the least of which is to have some sort of KM program. Although they can identify general best practices and encourage the use of KM tactics, KM standards must be flexible enough to permit an organization to develop a program that works for its specific business structure, mission, and internal culture.

8

And Finally...

We have just given you a *lot* of information about successful KM programs around the world and about how some programs died. We specifically asked our interviewees what advice they would give to a KM newbie. What they told us helped us identify the characteristics of a good KM program manager, and the skills and abilities which a program manager should have. "Knowledge management program manager" is a mouthful, so Paul came up with a term we will use to replace it: *knowledgeur*.

Entrepreneurs are people who start their own business, especially when they see a new opportunity. Similarly, a knowledgeur is someone who makes use of their or others' knowledge in one area and applies it for the beneficial use in another area or market. Often beginning as an inward facing or limited scope activity, it becomes more outward facing with the rise of communities and the subsequent need to collaborate outside of the organization.

1. Investigate
2. Navigate
3. Negotiate
4. Facilitate
5. Collaborate
6. Communicate
7. Curate
8. Celebrate

Figure 13
The eight "ates."

THE EIGHT "ATES"

After digesting the advice from our interviewees, we have identified eight skills that a successful knowledgeur should develop. These are what Paul likes to call the eight "ates" (see Figure 13). Specifically they are: investigate, navigate, negotiate, facilitate, collaborate, communicate, curate, and celebrate.

1. **Investigate:** As discussed in Chapter 2, it is important that the knowledgeur conduct three tasks:

    a. Identify and understand the stakeholders.

    b. Identify and prioritize the pain points.

    c. Define a baseline and metrics.

    When doing these tasks, the knowledgeur must take care not to take things at face value and should be able to look beyond the surface into the subtleties of how individual business units run and how they fit into and support the overall business mission and goals. Are you clear on the problem you are trying to solve and how that supports your business/organization? You will need to keep asking questions and evaluating what needs to be done and why. Note that you will have to do this periodically in order to stay current and make sure that your efforts remain relevant.

2. **Navigate:** The knowledgeur must identify the critical knowledge areas and knowledge assets in the organization and keep track of them. This can be done in many ways. One method is keeping a list of subject matter experts and where they are. Another could be a knowledge map of a group or department or, if you have the time and resources, for the entire organization. Regardless of how you do it, documenting the knowledge assets or knowledge flows for your organization can come in handy when identifying areas of knowledge risk, explaining why you are pursuing a given initiative, or even explaining to management why KM is needed at all. Even having a one-page diagram of how KM works might be helpful. People understand more quickly when they can see what you are talking about versus just hearing an explanation.

3. **Negotiate:** Most everything in an organization involves negotiation. The successful knowledgeur will be skilled at negotiating with stakeholders to get the time and resources needed to devise and implement effective KM initiatives. It will require anticipating and developing the answers to the question, "What's in it for me? (WIIFM)" for your stakeholders. If you have been diligent in your investigations noted above in item 1, this item will be easier.

4. **Facilitate:** So much of what a knowledgeur does involves facilitation. In many of the stories in Chapters 3 and 4, our interviewees noted that their success was attributed to KM team facilitation skills. Your knowledge of the stakeholders, pain points, and SMEs will enable you to facilitate connections, meetings, interactions, events, and communities. As you become known as a skilled and experienced facilitator, you will be sought after by workers and managers alike to help them improve performance, share knowledge, and improve process efficiency. Just remember to consider the WIIFM mindset.

5. **Collaborate:** Collaboration skills complement facilitation skills. You will most likely find yourself in a position to bring disparate groups together to solve business problems. The Big Peer Assist conducted by Airbus as described in Chapters 4 and 6 is a good example of how this skill can work. You may be the catalyst to help a business get unstuck.

6. **Communicate:** All of our interviewees noted that communication skills are key. Some suggested that knowledgeurs devote 25% or more of their time to communicating how KM supports the business, seeking feedback and keeping stakeholders informed at all levels. It might be a good idea to develop a communications plan and think about how to inform all levels of management as well as across the workforce. Having an elevator speech ready is also a good idea. Publicize KM successes and update them as often as possible. Let your stakeholders know what you are doing and why frequently.

7. **Curate:** People, in organizations and in their personal life, need to find 'stuff' (knowledge, data, and information). Much of the knowledgeur's role is about facilitating the creation, organization, and storage of relevant content and making it available for reuse. It is more than a librarian or information professional's role; we are talking about being a custodian of an organization's knowledge bases, helping to assemble and populate them, understanding what's important for the organization, and ensuring the right people get to see the right 'stuff' at the time they need it. The knowledgeur is in a unique position to identify and capture critical knowledge and to add value by identifying places in the organization where that knowledge could be used by others who may not be aware of its existence. In doing so, KM can optimize the use of an organization's knowledge and help it to function more effectively and efficiently.

8. **Celebrate:** The knowledgeur role can be a lonely one, especially when reporting lines and sponsors change. As noted in Chapter 5, KM is often not recognized as an important function within the organization. It is seen as a cost and the initial burst of enthusiasm for KM fades quickly if not periodically rejuvenated. Collect stories and be prepared to acknowledge contributions and celebrate successes. Don't be afraid to celebrate by speaking at KM symposia or conferences. Often organizations only recognize KM when you are seen as an authority on your subject in the outside world. Patricia's management sat up and took notice when her KM program received the 2010 MeriTalk Merit Award for streamlining government operations and she was repeatedly asked to speak about the NRC's KM program. Outside recognition not only increases the visibility of your KM efforts, it can also boost your own self confidence and help you renew your KM efforts.

Dead But It Won't Lie Down

Despite the decline of once-thriving KM programs, some continue and persevere.

Over a year after Patricia left, human resources finally appointed a new KM staff person who continues to hold periodic meetings. Although the NRC Knowledge Center is no more, they are now publishing KM documents to capture lessons learned from major events and efforts in the nuclear industry.

After the success at Lloyd's Register Marine to capture critical knowledge following the announcement of their office move, the KM staff has decreased to one. Yet that one person has derived a tool to enable managers to locate and identify key knowledge resources within the company located around the world.

In both these cases, funding is a bare minimum, staffing is minimal, and management support is almost non-existent, yet these small efforts persist. This is a testament to the dedication of KM staff who continue to attempt to help their organization do things more efficiently despite the apathy of the organization itself.

When we were putting this list of "ates" together, the list seemed overwhelming, but when Patricia sat and thought about it, she realized that in fact, she had done all of that. Would things have been better if Patricia had known all the things contained in this book? She will never know, but you have the chance to find out. Learn from those who went before you.... Now go out there and *do it!*

Appendix 1
The Consultant Dilemma

Establishing and maintaining an effective KM program is challenging. Imagine you've been asked to start a KM program or refresh one that's stuck. You have limited resources or no resources at all, and are permitted to go to a conference only if it is nearby or if it has low travel costs. So you attend KM conferences when you can, join LinkedIn groups, buy a few KM books, and hope that these activities will help you in your KM efforts. Chances are you will have to look for help with KM in your spare time because most of your daylight hours are spent putting out fires, engaging with stakeholders, and justifying the need for KM.

If you are really lucky you might have been given time and resources to develop a KM roadmap that supports the strategic direction of your business. You probably haven't and unless you work for a large consultancy / accounting practice, a big industrial concern, or a legal practice, yours will be a hand-to-mouth existence. You will learn on the job, end up being reactive rather than proactive, and wish there were more hours in the day to move the KM program forward.

Nevertheless, you will have some successes that you can share as anecdotes and some supporters who see the benefit of KM. But will you and your KM program survive management scrutiny when the budget gets tight and resources are scarce?

Earlier we suggested that "what you can measure you can manage." Few KM programs start with clearly identified and agreed benchmarks or baselines to measure KM program effectiveness. Here are some examples of clear metrics:

- Reduce by 25% the amount of time it takes to get new entrants up to speed and hence reduce training costs by 25%.

- Reduce by a third the average time it takes to produce a quality proposal to a client. (In some cases improved quality could improve the number of accepted proposals.)

- Become a knowledge hub, ensuring that whenever people want to know about "your" area they come to "you" for advice. This can be measured by the number, level, and complexity of requests made to your knowledge center.

All of this takes focus, time, and energy. With limited resources, how can you do it all? One answer is to seek external help. Hiring a KM professional can be challenging, but there are always consultants ready to help companies with whatever they need to get done. The thing is: how do you choose the right one for your need?

TYPES OF CONSULTANCY

Consultancy can take three forms:

- Strategic consultancy
- Operational or tactical consultancy
- Coaching and mentoring

Strategic consultancy often takes place before a program has begun or when it needs refreshing. Often driven by senior management, it involves analysis and assessment of your organization's knowledge capacity, needs, and risk. It is a frank appraisal of existing skills and provides recommendations and suggested actions to achieve measurable benefits—in effect assessing the capability of the current KM infrastructure.

The smart knowledge manager will assess the organization's knowledge capability and capacity before moving ahead with any operational actions. This is extremely difficult for an individual KM manager to do alone. Those with a budget may hire a contractor to do this work, recognizing the benefit of having an independent view.

Operational consultancy focuses on getting the organization and the people in it to perform tasks and/or change their ways of working. Typical examples include helping and encouraging people to capture anecdotes and stories as a way of knowledge capture, helping to set up and run communities of practice, and setting up and maintaining a knowledge base.

Coaching and mentoring are development techniques based on the use of one-to-one discussions with individuals and /or teams to enhance skills, knowledge, or work performance. Coaching tends to be more task specific and short term; mentoring takes place over a longer period with more generic aims. Typically this involves hiring someone with in-depth KM experience who can help you evaluate your efforts and do a "sanity check." It is always helpful to bounce your thoughts and ideas off of someone with an impartial perspective who has done it before—sort of an extension of this book.

This form of consultancy can be really valuable to organizations that want to develop a KM program in-house and recognize the need to draw on external expertise in designing, setting up, and maintaining it. This can be very helpful for programs that are "stuck."

SELECTING AND MANAGING THE CONSULTANT

Identifying, selecting, and working with consultants can be challenging. First, it is likely your consultant will have worked with a number of organizations and will have seen issues similar to yours. Second, the consultant might have different thoughts about how the assignment or task could be done and may challenge your way of thinking. Third, consultants might tell you what they think you want to hear instead of working with you to develop the best solution for your needs.

A good consultant will develop a solution considering your organization's context and explain it in terms that your organization can understand.

A great consultant may also tell you some unpalatable truths about your organization's readiness to set up a KM program or undertake operational KM tasks. In one case, Paul found that the core knowledge assets of an organization were not considered or accounted for in the overall company strategic plan. This gave the company's management pause, and they had to think long and hard about what to do.

When you think about working with a consultant, we suggest you follow several strategies:

- Be clear about what you are asking the consultant to do.
- Produce a scope of work that is specific but not too constraining with milestone deliverables.
- Produce an agreement that contains break clauses to permit evaluation of the work done and allow the client to determine whether to continue, change consultants, or issue a follow-on contract.
- Be sure the consultant has included in the proposal a risk register describing how setbacks will be dealt with (for example, changes in scope of work, unavailability of key personnel, unforeseen delays, and so on).
- Beware when hiring software consultants that they don't over engineer the solution. If you ask them for the time, make sure they don't build you an atomic clock.
- Assemble a steering group to oversee and evaluate the deliverables and act as champions for the work.

- Require regular periodic updates (F2F or video is best).
- Be prepared to own the outputs; don't subcontract your thinking.
- When making a selection, ask yourself, "Can I work with them?"
- And finally, don't be too ambitious and expect the consultant to solve every issue with one assignment.

FROM THE CONSULTANT'S VIEWPOINT

Having worked in the City of London for over two decades, Paul then embarked on a portfolio career as a consultant where he worked for a number of companies simultaneously. Paul has experienced both sides of the contractor–client fence and observes:

- Most people have a limited understanding of what it takes to respond to a call for a consulting proposal. In a recent example, three very well qualified consultants responded to a request for a proposal (RFP). It took a total of 25 person days to assemble the bid, write the 30-page document, develop the presentation, and deliver the pitch. Concurrently, similar groups were doing the same thing. When the bid was turned down, no explanation as to why was given.

- Organizations rarely meet the timetables they publish in their RFPs; however, they insist that prospective consultants respond immediately to their requests for additional information. In the above example, the RFP included inconsistencies that made writing the bid problematic. The client also failed to meet any of its published response times.

- Consultants (especially smaller ones) tend to over deliver. Those who have worked in KM before know what it takes to get stakeholder buy-in.

- One of the biggest challenges can be avoiding parroting a sponsor's preferred line back to them. A good consultant will be experienced at managing this situation.

- Another challenge is telling clients something they do not want to hear. A good consultant will also be experienced in managing this.

- In addition to periodic meetings, a good contractor will provide a "straw man," a draft of the report including proposed recommendations, and get agreement on the report format before finalizing anything.

Appendix 2
The Method or How We Came to Write This Book

WHO WE ARE

Patricia Eng

In 2007, Patricia was asked by NRC executives to create, design, and manage a knowledge management program for the U.S. Nuclear Regulatory Commission (NRC). Senior management knew they needed help in capturing expertise from staff. In 2004, NRC realized that they were going through a serious brain drain. They were losing roughly 4,000 person years of experience annually. At that time, more than 50% of NRC staff had less than five years of regulatory experience and the nuclear industry expressed its intent to submit more than 20 new power reactor license applications, many with new features and systems that had not been previously reviewed by the NRC. Requests for detailed technical reviews for new plant designs were increasing, expert staff were leaving in large numbers, and the remaining staff had little regulatory experience. Some had no licensing experience at all.

An NRC employee for almost 25 years, Patricia understood the need for a KM program but was unsure where and how to begin. During Patricia's KM journey, consultants claiming to be able to help her create a KM program called her weekly. Patricia was a one-woman show and had no budget or time to meet with all these consultants, let alone determine whether they could actually help her. So she just dug in and started experimenting. By her own admission she made many mistakes, but over time she met more experienced KMers at meetings and conferences and started to build her network. The tips and suggestions she got from these KMers helped her build a successful program. At the end of the first year of implementation, her efforts saved the NRC more than 37 million dollars in operating costs and earned NRC the 2010 MeriTalk Merit Award for streamlining U.S. government operations. Her efforts continued to save NRC money, 22 million in the second full year of implementation, and Patricia continued to work on expanding the KM program. She vowed to herself that someday she would write the book she had needed when she initially took on the KM program.

Paul Corney

Paul came at this from a very different perspective. After establishing one of the first knowledge management functions in the City of London in 1995, he spent the next 20 years as a global business advisor and consultant. Many of his assignments involved making better use of personal and organizational knowledge. Some were driven by a senior management team eager to solve a pressing business issue or crisis, a few were strategically driven, and a growing number were to mitigate risk or comply with emerging quality standards. Paul wanted to share his reflections and learnings from assignments conducted across four continents with the growing community of knowledge management professionals.

FORMING THE TEAM

Patricia and Paul met at a KM conference in the UK and realized that they were kindred spirits. They both felt strongly that the best advice and lessons learned would be gleaned from people who actually worked in their companies and organizations while developing the KM program. So Patricia and Paul decided to seek out experienced and successful KM practitioners from across their networks with proven track records and developed criteria for selecting interviewees.

INTERVIEWEE SELECTION CRITERIA

Paul and Patricia defined the criteria for selecting an interviewee as follows:

1. Had actually built a KM program for an organization they worked in (as opposed to consultants who were brought in to develop a KM program and then left)

2. Had spent at least two years in situ, preferably longer, on the program

3. Had served as the primary person responsible for the KM program

4. Could point to a clear return on investment (ROI), either monetary or in terms of productivity

5. Could speak to what constituted the ROI and other indicators of the KM program's success such as:

   a. Initial and periodic program resources and expenses

   b. Number of staff involved, both locally and in the "field"

    c. Quantifiable decrease in time to learn or certify and/or quantifiable increase in productivity

    d. Change in management attitude towards KM

6. Was willing to be interviewed about successes and failures

THE PROCESS WE USED TO WRITE THE BOOK

In creating this book Patricia and Paul used techniques knowledge managers use in their day-to-day work. First, we identified the purpose of the book. What were we trying to accomplish? Second, we applied the techniques discussed in Chapter 2. Who were our stakeholders, what were the pain points, and what sort of baseline or metrics were available for discussion that might be of help to others? Once that was done, we started working using the following techniques in specific areas:

Research and Capture

1. We defined the critical knowledge we were seeking.

2. We defined criteria for selecting people we might interview.

3. After reviewing our personal contacts, we also identified people who might know others who might know people who met our selection criteria.

4. We developed a stakeholder engagement process (questions to ask), and drafted an "invitation to participate" and an interviewee release form.

Analysis and Sense Making

1. We thought about our potential audience. What information did they need?

2. We thought about how to analyze, capture, and document the interviews and our observations.

3. We agreed to analyze the interviews separately and then compare our thoughts.

4. After the interviews were over, we met F2F to share our thoughts and observations and to decide on the book structure and content scope.

Production and Publishing

1. Paul proposed an online tool to house all of our discussions and project workings. Patricia complied but resisted the online tool.

2. Patricia found a publisher who was excited about our project and who agreed to publish it.

3. Interviewees were asked to review the portions of the book that described their programs and experiences with KM to ensure accuracy.

Research and Capture

The initial focus of the book was on knowledge capture and retention. As we progressed in our efforts, it became clear that our focus was too narrow. We found there was much to be learned and shared not only from the characteristics of successful and less successful KM programs but also from the thoughts and experiences of our interviewees. Even though we expanded our initial scope, the importance of capturing, retaining, and reusing critical knowledge remained a core component of our interviews, with sharing also playing a primary role in successful KM programs.

We used our own personal networks and contacts to identify the initial group of potential interviewees. We also asked our contacts whether they could suggest others who would be open to being interviewed and we gave them our selection criteria to help them identify potential interviewees for us. We used personal calls and communications instead of social media because we wanted a select group of individuals; we were concerned that a blanket request would not bring us the right people for our project.

In the beginning, we came up with a list of 10 interviewees that grew over time to 18. This growth was due in part to asking our first few interviewees whether they could suggest people they knew who might fit our criteria. Having been interviewed, several of them had great suggestions and the persons they referred us to were then interviewed for the book.

When people agree to give of their time it is important for them to know several things in advance: 1) what that time commitment is likely to be, 2) what the process will be, and 3) how much control they will have over what we say about them. We provided our interviewees with an overview of our project and described why we were doing it, the criteria we used to select them, and the questions that we would ask. After they agreed to be interviewed, we sent them the release form and noted that the interviews were averaging about an hour in length.

In the release form, we agreed to keep them updated on our progress and to provide a draft of the portion of the book that described their experiences with KM for their review before we submitted the manuscript to the publisher.

Our research and capture process was as follows:

- We sent a personal email 'request to participate' to each of our candidates.
- Once the candidates agreed to be interviewed, we sent the interview questions and release form.

- Patricia then set up a mutually agreeable date and time for the interview.

- Patricia conducted all the interviews, for consistency's sake, using online video conferencing tools such as Skype, WebEx, and GoToMeeting. Follow up communication was done by email.

- Patricia recorded the interviews and shared them with Paul via Dropbox.

We felt it important that each interviewee had time to prepare for the questions Patricia would pose (a copy of them appears on page 102). We appreciated that the interviewees were making time in their busy schedules to help us, so she was very flexible, often conducting interviews at unusual hours to accommodate the time differences and interviewee time constraints.

Because we hoped to draw on the interview material to illustrate our thoughts for this book, we knew it would be important to be able to use specific quotes and anecdotes. In most cases interviewees signed the release form with no questions. In a few cases, interviewees requested some additions and revisions to the form before signing. In the end we obtained signed release forms from all our interviewees.

Analysis and Sense Making

We assembled more than 40 hours of interviews. Knowing that we would have slightly different reactions to the interviews, we listened to the interviews separately and wrote up a summary of the interview and our observations. Coming from two different perspectives, our transcription styles and "noticings" (what we heard) were different. We knew that we wanted to write a practical book, and we knew that we needed to make sense of all this and be clear for our intended audience. To do this, we met F2F for two full days in January 2016 to review the interviews, go over our respective observations, and begin the process of creating a framework for the book. We highlighted quotes we felt illuminated points, and noted stories that we felt would bring each chapter to life and be useful for our readers.

We found the best way to do this was to write ideas and quotes on 'stickies' so we could move them around. It didn't take long before Patricia's sitting room wall and floor were covered in flip charts and sticky notes, as shown in Figure 14 on the next page. (It remained so until well after the manuscript was sent to the publisher.)

Figure 14 Using stickies to organize our thoughts
(Credit: P. Eng)

At the end of day two we had chapter headings, reconfirmed for whom the book was intended, and decided who was going to write what. As one of our interviewees noted: *"Most people don't know what they know because it is so ingrained."* So we thought that we should adopt good KM practice and made a commitment to write the "method" appendix you are reading. Patricia noted that it reads more complicated than it was to actually do.

Our analysis and sense making process was as follows:

- Patricia and Paul listened to the interviews and analyzed them separately.

- Paul and Patricia documented their summary and observations for each interview, and shared them with each other over the course of the project. Figure 15 shows how we worked collaboratively on chapters.

Figure 15 Patricia and Paul collaborating on the text.
(Credit: I. Rodwell)

- Patricia and Paul met F2F to go over their observations.

- Interviewees were asked to review and edit those portions of the book that described their KM program and their experiences before the manuscript went to the publisher.

Production and Publishing

Roughly six months into our efforts we chose our publisher, which influenced our F2F discussions on writing style, book framework, and content. Even so, we still had to define and write the chapters, get agreement on the quotes and attributions, and find images that might enhance the text.

Paul knew that we needed a collaborative platform for the content we would be generating and to record the conversations we would be having over the coming months. Despite a few glitches in the way content is stored (attachments appear at the foot of any text and need to be dragged and dropped to the relevant place in the text), we settled on Evernote.

Once we had drafted the text and obtained interviewee review and comment on our writing, we compiled the chapters and appendices into one file that we sent to a few trusted friends for review and comment (see Figure 16). After that, the draft went to the publisher for review, editing, typesetting, and whatever it is that publishers do to produce a book. We are sure that there will be some back and forth between us and the publisher, but for the most part, this is how we wrote the book.

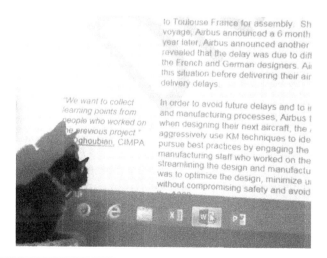

Figure 16 Patricia's cat helping to edit the text.
(Credit: P. Eng)

Exhibits

1. **Invitation to Participate:** The invitational email was adjusted and personalized for each prospective interviewee; here is the basic invitation.

   Subject: A personal invitation to participate in a book on proven knowledge capture and retention techniques

   We (Patricia Eng and Paul J. Corney) would like to invite you to participate in an effort to identify and highlight examples of good knowledge capture and retention practice that have made a real difference to your organization. Although there are many KM books out there, we feel that one about successful programs with tips and lesson learned from successful program managers would be useful and helpful to the KM community.

   Q. What are we asking for?

   A. An interview (in person or virtually, if that's easier) in which we will pose eight to ten questions about the initiative for which you have been responsible.

   Q. Why are we asking you?

   A. Because you have led an initiative in an organization to identify, capture, and share knowledge that resulted in a measurable return on the investment in time and resource.

   Q. What is the process?

   A. Once you've agreed to participate, Patricia will set up a time that is mutually convenient for the interview. In advance we will send you an outline of the areas we will be focusing on. You may have a copy of the recording if you wish and we will ask you to sign a waiver that we can use the material as part of the book.

   Q. What will we do with the material?

   A. We are asking questions with the aim of discerning patterns and success criteria from the material we generate. Each interview will be analyzed using a dialogue mapping and cataloguing technique. Snippets from each interview will be woven into various chapters. By the end of the year we will have consolidated the findings into a book. Obviously we will acknowledge your contribution and give you a copy of the book once it is published.

Q. What's in it for you?

A. A couple of things: a chance to share your experiences with other KM practitioner; a chance to benchmark your work against the other interviewees; global recognition of your work; and broader exposure.

Q. How long will it take?

A. The interview will take about an hour. We may need to contact you again if we need clarification of discussion points prior to publication. We are aiming to have the book published in 2016.

I hope you are able to join the dozen or so prominent organizations and practitioners who we have been/will be speaking to.

Please get back to us to let us know how we can contact you.

All the best, Paul/Patricia

2. **The Interview Questions Sent to the Interviewees:**

   Questions for Practical KM Interview Project – these are the basic questions.

   The actual interview may go into more detail in some areas and less in others, depending on how the discussion goes and if I am confused....

   1. Tell me about the circumstances and the drivers behind the original knowledge retention program and who was involved.
   2. How did you go about determining what knowledge to capture/retain?
   3. Give me a brief snapshot of how you went about it.
   4. What was the biggest challenge you had to overcome?
   5. How did you convince your management to go for it? 'Business Case?'
   6. What difference do you think it made to your organization? What was the actual return on investment?
   7. Is there a particular highlight you remember?
   8. If you had to do this over again, what would you do differently?
   9. What would you tell someone about to set out on a program to capture and retain knowledge?

Books Recommended by Our Interviewees

During our discussions, we asked interviewees about books they would recommend to a KMer. Here is the list:

Collison, Chris, *Learning to Fly: Practical Knowledge Management from Leading and Learning Organizations,* 2nd edition; Capstone (December 27, 2004), ISBN-10: 1841125091.

Davenport, Thomas and Prusak, Lawrence, *Working Knowledge,* 2nd edition; Harvard Business Review Press (May 2000), ISBN-10: 1578513014.

Gawande, Atul, *The Checklist Manifesto,* Reprint edition; Picador (January 4, 2011), ISBN-10: 0312430000.

Godin, Seth, *Tribes: We Need You to Lead Us,* 1st edition; Portfolio (October 16, 2008), ISBN-10: 1591842336.

Kahneman, Daniel, *Thinking Fast and Slow,* 1st edition; Farrar, Straus and Giroux (April 2, 2013), ISBN-10: 0374533555.

Krug, Steve, *Don't Make Me Think, Revisited: A Common Sense Approach to Web Usability,* 3rd edition; ISBN-10:0321965515.

Milton, Nicholas, R., *Knowledge Acquisition in Practice,* 1st edition; Springer London (May 1, 2007), ISBN-10: 1849966613.

Senge, Peter M., *The Fifth Discipline: The Art and Practice of The Learning Organization,* revised & updated edition; Doubleday (March 21, 2006), ISBN-10: 0385517254.

Stewart, Thomas A., *The Wealth of Knowledge: Intellectual Capital and the Twenty-first Century Organization;* Crown Business (August 19, 2003), ISBN-10: 0385500726.

Swenson, Keith D., *Mastering the Unpredictable: How Adaptive Case Management Will Revolutionize the Way That Knowledge Workers Get Things Done*, 1st Edition; Meghan-Kiffer Press (April 14, 2010), ISBN-10: 0929652126.

Van Winkelen, Christine and McKenzie, Jane, *Knowledge Works*, 1st edition; Wiley (August 15, 2011), ISBN-10: 1119993628.

Glossary

A350
The Airbus A350 is a long-range, twin-engine, wide-body jet airliner, the first Airbus aircraft with both fuselage and wing structures made primarily of carbon-fiber-reinforced polymer. Its variants seat 280 to 366 passengers in typical three-class seating layouts (i.e., economy, business, and first class).

A380
The Airbus A380 is a double-deck, wide-body, four-engine jet airliner manufactured by European Union manufacturer Airbus. It is the world's largest passenger airliner, and the airports at which it operates have upgraded facilities to accommodate it. Its variants seat up to 525 passengers in typical three-class seating layouts (i.e., economy, business, and first class).

Academy of Program and Project and Engineering Leadership (APPEL)
A training and development organization within NASA that provides employee training, hands-on development programs, and strategic communications to share project management and engineering lessons.

ACQuipedia
ACQuipedia serves as an online encyclopedia maintained by the Defense Acquisition University of common defense acquisition (procurement) topics. Each topic is identified as an article; each article contains a definition and a brief narrative that provides context and includes links to the most pertinent policy, guidance, tools, practices, and training. (https://dap.dau.mil/acquipedia/pages/about.aspx)

after action review (AAR)
A structured review or de-brief process conducted by participants and those responsible for a project or event for analyzing what happened, why it happened, and how it can be done better.

Airbus
A European consortium producing the Airbus family of passenger aircraft, a corporate jet, the beluga supertransport, and a military transport.

ARUP
A global independent firm of designers, planners, engineers, consultants, and technical specialists offering a broad range of professional services.

baby boomers
The demographic group born during the post–World War II baby boom, approximately between the years 1946 and 1964. This includes people who are between 52 and 70 years old in 2016, according to the U.S. Census Bureau.

best practice
A method or technique that has been generally accepted as superior to any alternatives because it produces results that are better than those achieved by other means, or because it has become a standard way of doing things. Sometimes a "best practice" is not applicable or is inappropriate for a particular organization's needs. A key strategic talent required when applying best practice to organizations is the ability to balance the unique qualities of an organization with the practices that it has in common with others.

BP, formerly British Petroleum
A British multinational oil and gas company headquartered in London, England. In 2012 it became the world's sixth-largest oil and gas company.

British Standards Institute (BSI)
BSI is the national standards body of the United Kingdom. BSI produces technical standards on a wide range of products and services and also supplies certification and standards-related services to businesses.

"C" suite
The executive suite; the cadre of executive managers including chief executive officer (CEO), chief operations officer (COO), and so on.

Cadbury Schweppes
Cadbury is a British multinational confectionery company wholly owned by American company Mondelez International (originally Kraft Foods). It is the second-largest confectionery brand in the world. Originally founded in 1824, Cadbury merged with drinks company Schweppes in 1969 becoming Cadbury Schweppes, but separated from Schweppes in 2008. It was purchased by Kraft in 2010. In 2012 Kraft's confectionery business, which included Cadbury, became Mondelez International.

CEO (chief executive officer)
The highest-ranking person in a company or other institution, ultimately responsible for making managerial decisions.

CGIAR: the Consultative Group for International Agricultural Research
A global partnership that unites organizations engaged in research for a food-secure future. It does this through a network of fifteen research centers known as the CGIAR Consortium of International Agricultural Research Centers, located around the globe. CGIAR research centers are generally run in partnership with other organizations including national and regional agricultural research institutes, civil society organizations, academia, and the private sector.

CIAT (Centro Internacional de Agricultura Tropical)
A not-for-profit research and development organization dedicated to reducing poverty and hunger while protecting natural resources in developing countries. Based in Palmira, Colombia, it is one of the fifteen specialized research centers of the Consultative Group on International Agricultural Research (CGIAR), and is also the headquarters for the CGIAR Research Program on Climate Change, Agriculture, and Food Security.

community of practice (CoP)
A group of people who share a concern or a passion for something they do and who learn how to do it better as they share information and interact regularly, either face to face or via online electronic meeting places.

corporate university
An educational entity that is a strategic tool designed to assist its parent organization in achieving its goals by conducting activities that encourage individual and organizational learning by improving on-the-job skills, focusing on company-specific proprietary knowledge, branding, and staff certification.

Defense Acquisition University (DAU)
A corporate university for the Defense Acquisition Workforce whose mission is to develop qualified acquisition, requirements, and contingency professionals who deliver and sustain effective and affordable warfighting capabilities. DAU provides formal courses and continuous learning modules to knowledge sharing assets, and provides consulting services in the area of acquisition and procurement for Department of Defense and military staff.

Deloitte
An international business consulting conglomerate consisting of independent firms around the world that provide audit, consulting, financial advisory, risk management, tax, and other related services to select clients. These firms are members of Deloitte Touche Tohmatsu Limited, a UK private company.

Digital Equipment
Digital Equipment Corporation, also known as DEC and using the trademark Digital, was a major American company in the computer industry from the 1950s to the 1990s. DEC was acquired in June 1998 by Compaq and subsequently merged with Hewlett-Packard (HP) in May 2002.

Dubai Government Excellence Program
An independent entity established in 1997 for the purpose of developing performance, concepts, practices, and techniques for application in the public sector in order to keep pace with modern updates in the administration and quality domain, and efficiently meet the changing requirements of the government sector in Dubai.

EFQM (European for Quality Management)
EFQM is a not-for-profit European membership foundation established in 1989 whose mission is to achieve sustainable excellence within the European Union by engaging leaders to learn, share, and innovate using the EFQM Excellence Model. (http://www.efqm.org/the-efqm-excellence-model)

elevator pitch
A succinct and persuasive sales pitch. In KM, a short summary used to quickly and simply demonstrate how KM has improved a process, product, service, organization, or event. It is based on the idea that it should be possible to deliver the summary in the time span of an elevator ride, approximately fifteen seconds to one minute.

face-to-face (F2F) communication
Communication that happens in real time with faces being visible. Face-to-face communication is no longer limited to in-person contact. Video conferencing is also a form of face-to-face communication, even though it uses technology to connect the participants.

gamification
The use of game design elements and principles in non-game contexts. For example, points earned for various actions in order to achieve a higher level of recognition to improve user engagement or interactions.

ground truth
Information provided by direct observation as opposed to information provided by inference, rumor, or hearsay.

Hewlett Packard
The Hewlett-Packard Company (commonly referred to as HP) was an American multinational information technology company headquartered in Palo Alto, California. It developed and provided a wide variety of hardware components as well as software and related services to consumers, small- and medium-sized businesses (SMBs), and large enterprises including customers in the government, health, and education sectors. Hewlett-Packard split the PC and printers business away from its enterprise products and services business in 2015, resulting in two publicly traded companies: HP Inc. and Hewlett Packard Enterprise.

HSCIC (Health and Social Care Information Center)
A business unit within the UK National Health Service, it serves as the national provider of information, data, and IT systems for commissioners, analysts, and clinicians in health and social care. It was renamed NHS Digital in the autumn of 2016.

IAEA (International Atomic Energy Agency)
The International Atomic Energy Agency (IAEA) is an international organization that seeks to promote the peaceful use of nuclear energy and to inhibit its use for any military purpose, including nuclear weapons. The IAEA was established as an autonomous organization on July 29, 1957, and reports to both the United Nations General Assembly and the UN Security Council.

IED (improvised explosive device)

A bomb constructed and deployed in ways other than in conventional military action. It may be constructed of conventional military explosives, such as an artillery round attached to a detonating mechanism. IEDs are commonly used as roadside bombs.

Information Technology (IT)

A department that focuses on computer operations and other information technology needs within a business. It typically controls what software and electronic tools a business may purchase and/or use.

Intellectual Property Office of Singapore (IPOS)

The Intellectual Property Office of Singapore (IPOS) is a statutory board under the Ministry of Law. IPOS advises and administers the intellectual property (IP) regime, promotes its usage, and builds expertise to facilitate the development of Singapore's IP eco-system. With IP fast becoming a critical asset in today's global markets, IPOS aims to be a trusted partner to empower all creators in our knowledge economy.

IRIS (International Railway Industry Standard)

An internationally recognized management system standard specific to the railway industry.

ISO (International Organization for Standardization)

ISO develops and publishes international standards. Although these standards are used to assess products and services for safety, reliability, and quality, ISO does not provide certification or conformity assessment services. A company seeking certification must hire an external certification body.

K4D (knowledge for delivery)

A recommendations management tool used within NHS Digital to propose ideas to improve NHS Digital processes. Suggestions may be submitted by anyone within NHS Digital and are vetted by a central review panel that decides whether to implement proposed changes.

KM maturity model

A tool for assessing the relative "maturity" of KM programs. There are many models out there, but most do not consider the differences and variances in how KM programs are designed and implemented. (Be wary of using a maturity model. It is better to determine what success will look like in your organization and how you will know that you are progressing [that is, how you will demonstrate to management that KM is effective and what difference it has made]. Then focus on how to improve what you are doing.)

knowledge
Knowledge is a familiarity, awareness, or understanding of facts, information, descriptions, or skills. Knowledge is acquired through experience or education by perceiving, discovering, or learning. Knowledge can refer to a theoretical or practical understanding of a subject. It can be implicit (as with practical skill or expertise) or explicit (as with the theoretical understanding of a subject); it can be more or less formal or systematic.

knowledge assets
Information or skills within a business that make it more valuable or competitive; the accumulated intellectual resources of an organization including information, ideas, insights, cognitive and technical skills, and capabilities. Some knowledge assets are held in databases, documents, policies and procedures, and patents; others reside within the heads of subject matter experts and are often not explicitly documented.

Knowledgeur (cf knowledge manager)
Someone who makes use of his/her/others' knowledge in one area and applies it for the beneficial use in another area or market. Initially focused internal to the organization, it expands outward with the use of communities of practice and the need for collaboration outside the organization. A discussion of the knowledgeur and the desired skill set is in Chapter 8.

knowledge management
Knowledge management (KM) is the process of creating, sharing, using, and managing the knowledge and information of an organization. It refers to a multi-disciplinary approach to achieving organizational objectives by making the best use of knowledge. Efforts typically focus on improved performance, competitive advantage, innovation, the sharing of lessons learned, and continuous improvement.

knowledge manager
A person assigned to manage the process of capturing, developing, storing, sharing, and effectively using knowledge in an organization.

knowledge map
A visual diagram or inventory of an organization's internal or external repositories or knowledge assets that show how these assets are related and connected. Knowledge maps can help identify potential areas of knowledge strength, weakness, and risk.

knowledge mapping

A process of surveying and associating items of information or knowledge, usually visually, so that the mapping itself creates additional knowledge. Determining, for example, where knowledge assets are and how knowledge flows within an organization. Information is gathered through interviews or meetings with stakeholders for a given area that is to be mapped. Discussion of this technique is in Chapter 2.

KPI (key performance indicator)

A measure of how effective a company is in achieving key business objectives. Organizations use KPIs to evaluate their success at reaching targets. Often success is simply the repeated, periodic achievement of some level of operational goal such as zero defects, positive customer satisfaction, and so on. Choosing the right KPIs requires a good understanding of what is important to the organization.

lesson learned

A lesson learned is knowledge or understanding gained by experience. The experience may be either positive or negative, as in a mishap or failure. A lesson learned should have a real or assumed impact on operations; should be valid in that it is factually and technically correct; and should be applicable in that it identifies a specific design, process, or decision that reduces the potential for failures and mishaps or supports positive results.

Lloyd's Register Marine

Lloyd's Register (LR) is a global engineering, technical, and business services organization wholly owned by Lloyd's Register Foundation, a UK charity dedicated to research and education in science and engineering. Founded in 1760 as a marine classification society, LR now operates across many industry sectors with some 9,000 employees based in 78 countries.

MAKE award (Most Admired Knowledge Enterprise)

Created in 1998 by Teleos (a British research company in knowledge management and intellectual capital areas), the award recognizes organizations that create shareholder wealth by transforming tacit and explicit enterprise knowledge and intellectual capital into superior products/services/solutions.

MeriTalk Merit Award

An award given to U.S. government organizations chosen for leading innovative programs utilizing technology to significantly improve agency transparency and accountability. MeriTalk is a partnership of public and private entities focused on improving U.S. federal government information technology operations.

Malaysia Petroleum Management (MPM)
MPM is a business unit within PETRONAS that serves as resource owner and contractor manager for all the hydrocarbon assets in Malaysia.

MTA (Metropolitan Transportation Authority)
The Metropolitan Transportation Authority is North America's largest transportation network serving a population of 15.3 million people in the 5,000-square-mile area fanning out from New York City through Long Island, southeastern New York State, and Connecticut.

NASA (National Aeronautics and Space Administration)
The National Aeronautics and Space Administration (NASA) is an independent agency of the executive branch of the United States federal government responsible for the civilian space program and aeronautics and aerospace research.

National Health Service
The publicly funded health care system serving the four countries within the United Kingdom: England, Ireland, Scotland, and Wales. The NHS is responsible for creating and maintaining comprehensive health and rehabilitation services for the prevention and cure of disease.

non-government organization (NGO)
A not-for-profit, voluntary citizens' group organized on a local, national, or international level.

NRC (U.S. Nuclear Regulatory Commission)
The U.S. Nuclear Regulatory Commission is responsible for the regulation and oversight of nuclear power plants and other commercial uses of nuclear materials, such as nuclear medicine, through licensing, inspection, and enforcement of NRC requirements.

NHS Digital
National Health Service Digital Division, formerly known as HSCIC, is the national provider of information, data, and IT systems for commissioners, analysts, and clinicians in health and social care in the UK.

Nuclear Decommissioning Authority (NDA)
NDA is a UK executive non-departmental public body within the Business, Energy & Industrial Strategy Department of the UK government. It is responsible for the safe and efficient clean-up of the UK's nuclear legacy including the decommissioning and demolishing of buildings as well as treatment and disposal of associated waste, both radioactive and conventional.

organizational memory
The accumulated body of data, information, and knowledge created in the course of an organization's existence. In a KM context, it also includes a capability to access experienced individuals who can speak with authority on such issues as needed.

pain point
In business, a real or perceived issue that hinders efficient or effective processes or communications often adversely affecting productivity.

PA (personal assistant)
An individual assigned to support an executive's administrative and logistical needs.

peer assist
A tool that supports 'learning before doing' processes in which advice is sought from an individual or a group that has previously done something similar. It usually is done in a face-to-face meeting where people with relevant knowledge and experience meet with those wishing to do a similar project or task. These meetings vary in length from a few hours to a few days, depending on the scope of the effort or project and the complexity and depth of the conversations.

PETRONAS (Petroliam Nasional Berhad)
The national oil and gas company of Malaysia, they serve as custodian for Malaysia's natural gas and oil resources and are responsible for developing and managing these resources.

pilot project
A small-scale preliminary effort or study conducted in order to evaluate the feasibility, time, cost, adverse events, and potential effects of a proposed change to a process or procedure. The goal of the pilot project is to predict the impact of a full-scale effort and to determine whether such full-scale implementation is worthwhile.

Port of Antwerp
Located in Belgium, it is Europe's second-largest seaport and can accommodate the largest of cargo ships.

repeat-back communications
The practice of restating what you think someone said in your own words to see whether you actually understood the message. This technique lets the speaker know whether his or her communication was effective and ensures that you both understand what is being communicated.

results-based management
A management strategy that uses feedback loops to achieve strategic goals. All people and organizations that contribute directly or indirectly to the result map out their business processes, products, and services in order to show how they contribute to the outcome.

retention of critical knowledge (ROCK)
A program developed and maintained by Shell Oil to identify, capture, and retain expert knowledge. The ROCK program consists, in part, of interviews with knowledge workers that capture and record their skills in the Shell Wiki, cited as the largest corporate Wiki according to Accenture in 2011. In addition to ROCK, Shell maintains internal KM communities that have generated 'audited savings of $300–$400 million dollars per year.' (http://oilit.com/2journal/2article/HTMLArticles/1104_12.htm)

RFP (request for proposal)
A type of bidding solicitation by which an organization announces that funding is available for a particular project or program and invites companies to submit bids for the project's completion.

ROI (return on investment)
In classic terms, return on investment is a performance measure used to evaluate the efficiency of an investment or to compare the efficiency of a number of different investments. ROI measures the amount of return relative to the investment's cost. In the investment world this is calculated as follows: ROI = (net profit/cost of investment) x 100. In KM terms, it is less well defined. Often people speak in terms of time saved or money saved.

SCARF®
The SCARF model is a brain-based framework designed to enhance self and social awareness and improve the quality of daily interactions. The model provides a means of bringing conscious awareness to our approach when collaborating with and influencing others. SCARF stands for Status, Certainty, Autonomy, Relatedness and Fairness. (https://neuroleadership.com/solutions/licensing/)

Sellafield
Sellafield Ltd is the company responsible for safely decommissioning the UK's nuclear legacy, for fuel recycling, and for managing low, high, and intermediate level nuclear waste activities on behalf of the Nuclear Decommissioning Authority.

Shell
Shell Oil Company is the United States-based subsidiary of Royal Dutch Shell, a multinational "oil major" of Anglo-Dutch origins, which is among the largest oil companies in the world.

silver bullet
We use the term 'silver bullet' to refer to an action that cuts through complexity and provides an immediate solution to a problem. The allusion is to a miraculous fix, otherwise portrayed as 'waving a magic wand.' It originally came from the notion that a bullet made of silver is necessary to kill a werewolf.

Skype
Skype is an online application that provides video chat and voice call services using the Internet.

SME (subject matter expert)
A subject matter expert (SME) or domain expert is an authority in a particular area or topic.

stakeholder
A person or group with an interest or concern in something such as a topic, subject, or process.

WIIFM (What's in it for me?)
An acronym that describes the value proposition, the thing or statement that helps people decide whether what you are offering or asking them to do is worth their money, time, and participation.

Index

WHY ASQ?

ASQ is a global community of people passionate about quality, who use the tools, their ideas and expertise to make our world work better. ASQ: The Global Voice of Quality.

FOR INDIVIDUALS

Advance your career to the next level of excellence.

ASQ offers you access to the tools, techniques and insights that can help distinguish an ordinary career from an extraordinary one.

FOR ORGANIZATIONS

Your culture of quality begins here.

ASQ organizational membership provides the invaluable resources you need to concentrate on product, service and experiential quality and continuous improvement for powerful top-line and bottom-line results.

www.asq.org/why-asq

ASQ
The Global Voice of Quality

ASK A LIBRARIAN

Did you know?

Quality Resource contains a wealth of knowledge and information available to ASQ members and non-members.

A librarian is available to answer research requests using ASQ's ever-expanding library of relevant, credible quality resources, including journals, conference proceedings, case studies and Quality Press publications.

ASQ members receive free internal information searches and reduced rates for article purchases.

You can also contact the Quality Information Center to request permission to reuse or reprint ASQ copyrighted material, including journal articles and book excerpts.

For more information or to submit a question, visit asq.org/quality-resources.

ASQ
The Global Voice of Quality